PIONEER PHOTO
New!!!
Cloth Frame Scrapbooks

12" x 12" *and* 8" x 8"
Top Loading Post Bound

Archival ACID FREE Photo Safe

Standard Colors	*Bright Colors*	*Earth Tone Colors*	*Trend Colors*	*Baby Colors*
Apple Red	**Bright Pink**	**Champion Burgundy**	**Tangerine Orange**	**Dreamy Pink**

Sky Blue	**Cobalt Blue**	**Regal Navy**	**Turquoise Blue**	**Heavenly Blue**

Sage Green	**Citrus Green**	**Biscotti Beige**	**Soft Yellow**	12" x 12" MB-10CBFB *and* 8" x 8" MB-88CBFB

Deep Black	**Grape Purple**	**Chocolate Brown**	**Misty Lilac**	*White* **Cloud White**
				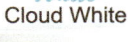 
12" x 12" MB-10CBF *and* 8" x 8" MB-88CBF	12" x 12" MB-10CBFS *and* 8" x 8" MB-88CBFS	12" x 12" MB-10CBFE *and* 8" x 8" MB-88CBFE	12" x 12" MB-10CBFT *and* 8" x 8" MB-88CBFT	12" x 12" MB-10CBFW *and* 8" x 8" MB-88CBFW

Pioneer Photo Albums, Inc.
(800) 366-3686 • (818) 882-2161 • Fax: 8188826239 • pioneer@pioneerphotoalbums.com

PIONEER

FROM THE EDITOR

I love a good story. My favorite form of relaxation is curling up with a really good book and getting so involved in the plot that I can't put it down. It's a family pastime, too—over the years our family has worn out our comfortable rocking love seat as we've curled up and read together. Reading a story is one of the wonderful, simple pleasures of life. Stories take you into a completely different world, open your imagination and enrich your life. And that is just what mini albums are—wonderful stories. Only they're made up of your own memories and illustrated with your own photos, which makes them the best stories of all.

Mini albums are the perfect way to record your life's experiences. You can fill them with special occasions, places you have visited, people who are dear to you, or your favorite things. They are the ideal place to record your feelings, a typical day in your life, or describe why you love someone. They can be detailed and fancy, or straightforward and simple. They give you the chance to become author as well as publisher; your mini album is your very own completed work of art.

We have collected a few of our favorite mini albums submitted to us by our readers and are very excited to share them with you. With these handy ideas at your fingertips, you're all set to make tons of fun mini albums of your own. So the next time you want to curl up with a good book, pull out one of your mini albums and read it to someone you love. Memories can be elusive, but if you bundle them up in a mini album, you can take them out to enjoy time and time again!

Pam

Pam Baird
EDITOR-IN-CHIEF

Journaling
your stories
with Kara Henry

ISBN-10: 0-9705613-7-7
ISBN-13: 978-0-9705613-7-4

51795

9 780970 561374

scrapbook TRENDS

Every life has stories to tell—and every scrapbooker wants to tell them. Journaling expert Kara Henry has a deep conviction about the importance of journaling in scrapbooks, and she has gathered hundreds of great ideas that will take your own stories from elusive memory to the written word. Prompts, suggestions, and tips for more meaningful journaling will help you find the right words to scrapbook everything from everyday events to special occasions, from relationships to the things that make you laugh. Go from writer's block to a scrapbook full of memories—share your stories!

Publisher Chad Harvie

Editor in Chief Pam Baird

Assistant Editor Tammy Morrill

Editorial Staff
Alisha Gordon, Kara Henry, Jana Johnson, Paige Taylor

Art Director Amy Noorda

Design
Jeri Huish, Linda Nelson, Hannah Craner, Linnette Deason

Cover Photography Kaycee Leishman

Photography
Mio Watanabe, Linda Nelson

Retail Sales
Jan Rudd
888-225-9199 x12
janr@scrapbooktrendsmag.com

Newsstand Distribution & Large Accounts
David Ross
888-225-9199 x 14
david@scrapbooktrendsmag.com

Subscriptions/Customer Service
Sarah Dalsing, Janis Kunz, Jessica Swain

Shipping/Receiving
Tina Gonzales, Sean Curran

Internet Customer Service
support@scrapbooktrendsmag.com

Advertising
Amber Hall
888-225-9199 x14
amberh@scrapbooktrendsmag.com

Scrapbook Trends Magazine is published 12 times
a year by Northridge Media, LLC.
P.O. Box 1570 Orem, Utah 84059-1570
phone **888-225-9199** fax **801-225-6510**
e-mail: support@scrapbooktrendsmag.com
www.scrapbooktrendsmag.com

Subscriptions 1-888-225-9199
6 issue subscription: $49.95
12 issue subscription: $84.95
18 issue subscription: $124.95
24 issue subscription: $159.95
Please call for international rates.

Please send address changes to:
Northridge Media
P.O. Box 1570
Orem, Utah 84059-1570
or e-mail: support@scrapbooktrendsmag.com

Please send reader submissions to:
submissions@scrapbooktrendsmag.com

CONTENTS

features

sections

101 mini ALBUM IDEAS

In the mood to make a mini album? Here are 101 ideas to jump-start your imagination.

step-by-step albums for kids

Taking a Bath
Getting Ready for the Day
Getting Ready for Bed
How To Get Out of Trouble
How To Make a Mess

family

Time Capsule
(headlines, gas prices, family stats, etc.)
Tribute to Mom/Dad
Family Profiles/Our Kids
Family Portraits through the Years
Names
The Grandkids
States We've Visited
Vehicles We've Owned
Vacation
Family Reunion
Medical Records
(immunization dates, etc.)

home

Our Address(es)
Our Home, Room-by-Room
The Garden

Remodelling—Before & After
Our Favorite Meals & Recipes
Fine China/Table Settings
My Dream *(Home, Kitchen, etc.)*

outings

A Day at the Zoo/Carnival
Amusement Park Fun
A Trip to the Beach
Camping Trip
4-Wheeling/Biking
National Parks
Road Trips
Going on a Walk

kids

Funny Faces
Favorite Foods/Toys
Alphabet
Numbers
Friends
Birthdays
The Funny Things You Say
Baseball/Dance/Soccer/Gymnastics
(extracurricular)

babies

Cute Little Outfits
12 Months
Daily Routines
Baby's Firsts/Milestones
Baby Parts *(toes, fingers, etc.)*
Week-by-Week
Silly Expressions

holidays

First Pictures of the New Year
Why I Love My Valentine
My Country 'Tis of Thee
Halloween Costumes through the Years
Thanksgiving Cookbook/Menu
8 Days of Hanukkah
12 Days of Christmas
Christmas Lists
Christmas Presents
Holiday Traditions
Holiday Card Photos
(ones you receive or yours through the years)
Favorite Holiday Treats

heritage

Family Traits
Timeline of Your Life
Family Tree
Heritage Recipes
Heirlooms
I Look Up To You

a day in the life of . . .

My Son/Daughter
My Significant Other
My Pet
My Kitchen
My House
Me

special occasions

High School Graduation
Prom
The Big Game
Baby Shower
The Day You Were Born
The Story of Us/How We Met
Bridal Shower
Shopping for the Wedding Dress
Wedding Guest Sign-In book
The Wedding Reception

all about me

*You could also apply these ideas to
a friend or family member.*

Current Events From The Year I Was Born

High School Memories

My Daily Routines

Soundtrack to My Life

Celebrity Crushes through the Years

10 Quirks

If I Had a Million Dollars

My Personality *(quiz answers)*

Things to Do By the Time I'm *(30, 50, 100…)*

My Favorite… (*Books, Quotes, Movies, TV Shows,
Places to Eat, etc.*)

Before & After *(weight loss, makeover, etc.)*

My Hobbies

Things I Make *(quilts, crafts, etc.—show pictures
and who you gave them to)*

Hairstyles through the Years

What's In My Closet *(literally or figuratively!)*

Things I Can't Live Without/Things I Use Everyday

My Goals

Best Friends

The Hats I Wear

Places I Want to Visit

What I Want to Be Remembered For

BE create NOW TODAY MINE
*day voice time explore DAILY
great JOURNEY GO

CONNECTE
BY LOVE

WHAT I see

a photo journal
of August 2006
...
marielambert

"This is one of my most treasured albums. I started out with the simple idea of taking one photo a day for a month and scrapping a page about that photo. Originally, it was a way to commit to being creative every day, but it ended up being a wonderful chronicle of my family's life. In the beginning, I was looking for anything to photograph, but by the end of the month I was looking for the significant thing that happened each day, such as taking my daughter shopping for kindergarten uniforms, making pizza with the girls, or watching my daughter line up crayons on the floor. I realized all these little things are the things that make up our life together."

WHAT I SEE by Marci Lambert

Album is 6" square

Cardstock: Bazzill Basics; Patterned paper: 7 Gypsies, Basic Grey, cherryArte, Hambly Studios, KI Memories, My Mind's Eye, Paper Loft, Paper Studio, Provo Craft, Scenic Route Paper Co., SEI; Overlays: Hambly Studios; Brads: Making Memories; Ribbon: Scrapworks; Flowers: Prima; Rub ons: 7 Gypsies, Chatterbox, KI Memories, Making Memories; Stickers: 7 Gypsies, American Crafts, Die Cuts with a View, Doodlebug Design, Heidi Swapp, Making Memories, Paper Studio; Gaffer tape: 7 Gypsies; Journaling spot, edge distresser: Heidi Swapp; Stamps: EK Success, Making Memories, Hobby Lobby, Technique Tuesday; Ink: ColorBox, StazOn, Tsukineko; Paint: Heidi Swapp, Making Memories; Pen: Uni-Ball Signo; Font: Bulky Refuse, from dafont.com; Other: Staple, file folder labels, photo corners, ric rac, paint chip, index cards, masking tape

This album was a chance for Marci to play creatively, and she scrapped almost all the pages on the day she took the picture. For her base pages, she cut sixteen 6" squares of white cardstock, and used the front and back to keep the book from getting too bulky. To challenge herself, Marci mainly limited herself to whatever scraps happened to be on her desk when she sat down to make the page, but she used the same stamps throughout for consistency. Each page took anywhere from 20 minutes to an hour to come together.

JUST RIGHT

FAVORITES BEST MOST GREATEST TOO MUCH NOT YOU

02 august

— we painted the
— Kitchen "Burgalow"
— Gold." Much better
— than The orange.

CONNECTED BY LOVE

AWAY
ADVENTURE
EXCURSION
ROAM

august **03**

Chuck E. Cheese today.
OMG, I hate this place.
But they love it.

SAFARI

august **10**

DEVOTED
treasures
active
PLAYGROUND
have a ball

When you are three,
sometimes the best
thing you can do is
to line up your new
crayons on the floor
and make a train.
Then you pick them
up and do it all
over again. because
you are three.

PLAY

the thrill of VICTORY

practice   never give up

ATTITUDE
EXPLORE

challenge   SHE'S ALL THAT
PROJECTED GROWTH
              determination   adorable

commitment

CONNECTED BY LOVE

audrey decided to
sample the chocolate
cheesecake i made
for my girls' night
out scrap night.

wHen **Toddlers**
aTtack

august **11**

22 august — MEMOIRS

WELCOME BACK ELEMENT

Margret's first day of kindergarten was great! no one cried, not even mommy!

3456

Qq Rr Ss Tt Uu Vv Ww Xx

august **23**

if i had a scrap intern, the first thing she would do is clean up my art room desk

MEMOIRS

august **26**

we had a great time at the Shaw's house tonight. after dinner the girls put on a fashion show. they all played so well together.

daddy let you pick out a prize at the Target $1 spot and you picked these cups. you are thrilled with them!

27 august

 Thanksgiving weekend is a special time of year for our family when we reflect on our blessings, and I wanted to create a mini album to celebrate all the things I'm thankful for. I used a different color for each theme to symbolize what they mean to me—for example, I used blue for a page about me because it's my favorite color, green for my children to symbolize youth and energy, red for love, etc. I've found that the easiest and quickest way to complete a mini album is to find a theme and style and repeat it throughout."

THANK YOU by Sonja McLean

Album is 4" square
Patterned paper: Basic Grey, Crate Paper, My Mind's Eye; Eyelets: Craft supply; Brads: Making Memories; Ribbon: American Crafts, Creative Imaginations, May Arts; Flowers: Prima; Tags, metal binder ring: Office supply; Rub ons: American Crafts, Basic Grey, Making Memories; Stickers: Rebecca Sower Nostalgiques; Ink: Ranger; Pen: Sakura; Font: Autumn Leaves Worn Machine, from twopeasinabucket.com

Sonja's cardstock album is bound with a metal ring using a silver eyelet as the hole reinforcer. She used monogrammed metal-rimmed tags as page separators and backed each one with a foam square and cardstock circle to help them stand out from the page.

 One day I heard a song on the radio that made my heart skip a beat—it reminded me of falling in love years ago. Right then, I decided to make a list of songs that define moments in my life. That list (along with the stories) turned into a blog post, and a fellow scrapbooker commented that it would make a great mini album. And so the seed was planted. About a year later, I actually began creating the album and it has been one of the most fun projects I have ever worked on! I think I had a smile on my face the entire time because of the happy memories I associate with each and every song. My favorite thing about this album is that it came from my heart—it shares my story, my heart, my soul, and that is why I scrapbook."

THE SOUNDTRACK OF MY LIFE by Megan Thurman

again i go uNoticed

The first year of our marriage was not an easy year. Within two weeks, I got married & left all my friends and family to live in California with my new husband. It was a difficult transition to say the least. Before moving, my little brother gave me a Dashboard CD, and I listened to it constantly. All of the songs resonated with me, but this one in particular. This song, while definitely not a sappy love song, will always remind me of that first year.

have faith

-dashboard confess

"I'll wait until tomorrow...

...maybe we'll be

better then..."

2000

You'll always be special to me

special

1995

-the Cranbem

TOGETHER

I met him in July 1995 on a mission trip, and we quickly hit it off. By the end of the summer, we had gone on a few dates, and I had completely fallen for him. He left for college, and as much as I hoped we had a future, I was doubtful. But then the letters started. And the phone calls. And finally, after a few weeks, a visit. We went to the park, and on the way, he slid a tape into the player, and music filled the car. We sat in silence, holding hands. The song said everything he wanted to say but couldn't. That was it. the moment I knew we had something special. That something special grew into the love of my life.

Album is 6" square Cardstock: The Paper Company; Patterned paper: Piggy Tales; Metal letters: Queen & Co.; Ribbon: American Crafts; Ghost letters: Heidi Swapp; Buttons: Bag of Buttons; Sequins: Hobby Lobby; Punches: EK Success; Rub ons: Basic Grey, EK Success; Stickers: 7 Gypsies, American Crafts, Doodlebug Design, Making Memories, Three Bugs in a Rug; Stamps: Autumn Leaves; Ink: Clearsnap, Stampabilities; Pen: Zig; Photography: Megan Thurman, Derek Thurman, Sarah Taylor, Kaminski Photography

Megan created her album from chipboard covers, cardstock pages and bound it with strings of ribbon. She kept a theme throughout using cut out flowers and other elements from the Piggy Tales Little Red Riding Hood Collection of patterned paper.

> This album I created for my oldest daughter was an effort to capture the everyday moments of her life. I wanted to include who her friends are now and her experience in going to a new school. My favorite page is 'My Wish.' I wanted to let Shelby know how this song made me think of her and how it put into words the way I feel now. I also included memorabilia from her cheerleading and tried to capture the things that she achieves."

S by Dedra Long

Album is 7 ½" square

Album, stickers, decorative tape: 7 Gypsies; Patterned paper: 7 Gypsies, Creative Imaginations, Foof-a-La; Notepad: Target; Die cuts: Bam Pop, Foof-a-La; Chipboard: Heidi Swapp, Technique Tuesday; Acrylic: KI Memories; Buttons: Foof-a-La, Swarovski; Crystals, award ribbons: Swarovski; Rub ons: 7 Gypsies, Autumn Leaves, Foof-a-La; Ribbon: Jo-Ann Scrap Essentials; Ghost flower, colored pencils: Heidi Swapp; Stamps: Autumn Leaves, Fontwerks, Jo-Ann Scrap Essentials, Making Memories, Sassafras Lass; Ink: ColorBox, StazOn, Tsukineko; Pens: Ranger, Zig

Dedra used folded decorative tape as a border around the grid on her album cover. The inside pieces are torn for a more jagged feel. Underneath, the pictures are covered with a transparency for a clean, glossy look that also doubles as a protective layer. Try using foam squares to help the pictures stand out from a patterned background.

state 12.10.06

MY WISH

Are you a... *Stampaholic?*

No one here will judge you if you stash your stamps in unlikely places around the house, feel inexplicable urges to stamp, or even start stamping before noon. It's OK—we understand. (This is not an intervention.)

WWW.GREENGRASSSTAMPS.COM

green grass stamps

 I made these albums as gifts for my parents and in-laws for Christmas. My daughters have four sets of grandparents, most of whom live out of town, so it's hard for them to attend all our celebrations. These mini albums share some of our favorite memories from 2006, including holidays, birthdays and special occasions. I created the albums using one digital scrapbook kit ("Merry & Bright" by Heather Roselli, from thedigichick. com), so it was a snap to print four sets of pages to create multiple albums. I chose to make accordion albums because they're compact, but also display nicely on a shelf."

2006 YEAR IN REVIEW by Ashleigh Stevens

Album created digitally in Adobe Photoshop 8.0 Album is 6" square Digital papers, stamps, other elements: Heather Roselli (Merry & Bright kit), thedigichick.com; Digital chipboard: Atomic Cupcake; Ribbon: Michaels; Font: Walt Disney Script, from momscorner4kids.com; Accordion album with box, snowflake charm: Oriental Trading Company; Photography effect: Purty Pics POP2 Action by Holly McCaig

This accordion album measures 6" square and is 12 pages long, perfect for one year's photo highlights.

 I created this album so that I could have something small to display on our coffee table during the holidays. My daughters like to look at the pages and reminisce about previous Christmases—it is the perfect size for little hands! Each year I plan to add new pages to this album. I used Doodlebug 'paper frills' on most of the pages, and also created some frills of my own using decorative scissors (glad I never got rid of those!) and a small hole punch."

Album is 9 ⅛ x 3 ⅜"

Cardstock: Die Cuts with a View; Patterned paper: KI Memories; Metal embellishments, tags: Making Memories; Ribbon, buttons: Craft supply; Chipboard: Scrapworks; Punches: Provo Craft; Die cuts, rub ons, stickers: KI Memories; Paper frills: Doodlebug Design; Stamps: My Sentiments Exactly; Scalloped scissors: Fiskars, Provo Craft; Pen: Sakura; Album: SEI; Photography: Laura Ping, Dustin Nakamura

tree
joy
christmas

Charlie Brown
[lighTs aNd disPlay]

Kenny bought these Charlie Brown figures a few years ago. I made this display in the girls' room with lights. Kendal & Chase love to play with them. They also have a lil tree!

this year instead of making a gingerbread house, we decided to make a gingerbread train. we had seen on in a magazine, but then I found this kit at the store. the girls ate more candy than went on the train.

GIN GER **bread**
ry * cookies *
mories * b *train*

gifts

Christmas
morning

As Kendal gets older, she is really starting to get excited about Christmas. this year she is showing Chase the "ropes." this year Kendal asked for and received a "Dora the Explorer" house. Kendal picked out a castle game for chase, all by herself!

pumpkin snowmen

We made our "pumpkin snowman" again this year. this time we decided to make an entire snowman family. Chase played with the pom poms while Kendal painted the pumpkins while I took a picture of the girls with their pumpkins. the picture turned out so cute, that we decided to use it in our Christmas card.

We

are so

blessed to have

you spend your

first Christmas as part

of our family. We couldn't

ask for a better gift than you!

1st

cupid donner blitzen rudolph dasher dancer prancer

dasher dancer prancer vixen comet cupid donner blitzen rudolph dasher dancer prancer

Christmas

Dustin uses a variation on the traditional red and green Christmas colors by largely using lime greens and pinks for this album. She creates a feeling of Christmas throughout right down to journaling in the shape of a Christmas tree. Notice a journaling tag is hidden behind their family picture on page 27.

I made this album for my Mum on her 50th birthday. We took her out for dinner to her favorite restaurant and I snapped some pictures while we were there waiting on our meal. That night, I had the pictures developed and made the album, then presented it to her the next day—she loved it! I wanted her to have something to remind her of such a special day, something she could share with family when they come to visit."

CELEBRATE by Michelle Cathcart

Album is 4 ¾ x 5 ½"
Patterned paper: Crate Paper; Brads: Making Memories; Chipboard: KI Memories; Flower: Poppy Ink; Buttons: Dress It Up; Thread: DMC; Rub ons: Basic Grey, Junkitz, Royal & Langnickel; Pen: Zig; Album: Die Cuts with a View

"This needed to come together quickly, so I kept it fairly simple. I used the same design for each page and added some simple embellishments. The buttons were hand-stitched in place, and for the cover, I applied a sheet of birthday rub ons to patterned paper. Originally all the pictures were in color, so I changed them to black and white to coordinate better with the patterned paper."

AHOY MATEY by Christina Padilla

"Pirates have been so popular lately, not just in movies and fashion, but scrapbooking as well. We threw a pirate-themed birthday for my son, and after seeing Hambly Studio's pirate papers and overlays, I just had to make a mini book about the party! I included fun pictures from the party, the handmade flag invitation and pirate themed accessories that were given to the children. The paper and overlays were perfect for the book."

Album is 7 x 12"

Cardstock: Bazzill Basics; Patterned paper: Hambly Studios, Karen Foster Design, Sandylion; Ribbon: May Arts, Offray; Chipboard: Heidi Swapp (frame), Scenic Route Paper Co.; Flowers: Petaloo; Acrylic, credit card tag, photo corners: Heidi Swapp; Die cuts: Daisy D's, My Mind's Eye; Button: SEI, Westrim Crafts; Rub ons: Hambly Studios; Stickers: Creative Imaginations, Doodlebug Design, Heidi Swapp, L'il Davis Designs, Making Memories, Provo Craft, Scenic Route Paper Co.; Decorative tape: 7 Gypsies, Heidi Swapp; Staples: Making Memories; Leather strip: L'il Davis Designs; Pirate eye patch, map, beads: Party supply; Stamps: 7 Gypsies, Hero Arts, L'il Davis Designs, Purple Onion Designs; Ink: Ranger, StazOn; Paint: Plaid, Ranger; Pen: Sharpie, Slick Writer, Uni-Ball Signo; Other: Pirate party hat, rings

In her album, Christina details everything about her son's pirate-themed birthday party. She includes a copy of the invitation, a pirate party hat (cleverly doubling as a layout background), pictures of his presents, guests, decorations, cake, etc. Such a clever way to help him remember everything about his fun 3rd birthday party!

Destination ESCAPE USA rela

Journey through

9 -to- 17
SEPT
2006

WALKING SOUTHER

Beach

travelers

Voyage

touring

NORTHERN

country

Explore

FLY Beauty

CALIFORNIA

"This album was made on a crazy trip, where we visited seven cities in eight days. (I think I got 20,000 frequent flier miles in one week!) It was a great experience, but if I hadn't written down what we did each day, I never would have been able to remember it all. I also loved having a place to include all my travel memorabilia—boarding passes, claim tickets, etc."

9 TO 17 SEPT 2006 by Allison Flynn

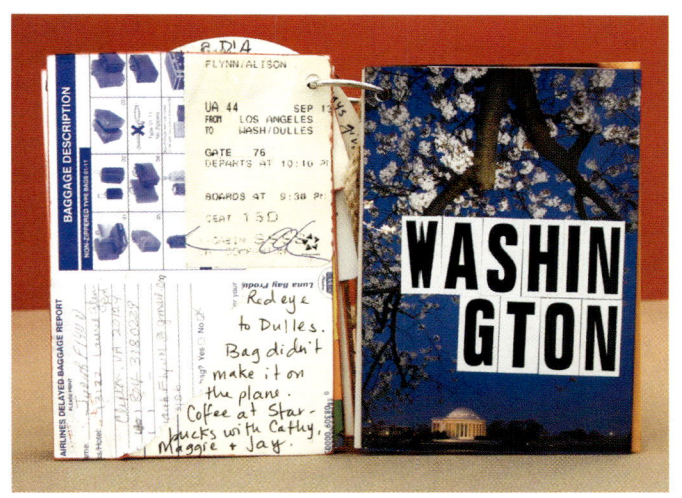

Album is 4 x 6"
Patterned paper: Karen Foster Design; Chipboard, hole punch: Office supply; Rub ons: Autumn Leaves; Stickers: Avery, Making Memories; Stamps: Junkitz; Ink: ColorBox; Pen, highlighter: Stabilo; Other: Postcards, metal ring, ephemera, string

Allison knew she would be moving around a lot and didn't have room to carry many supplies. So she put together a small kit with just a hole punch, metal ring, a stamp, ink and a pen. She then bought postcards in all the cities she visited and journaled on the backs, leaving room for some photos later. Newspapers and other memorabilia help make a complete picture of her trip.

"My zoo book is very special to me. My niece and her sons come to visit us from Alaska every summer, and we look forward to their visit all year long. The boys love to go to the zoo in Seattle and I adore taking photos of them. It's a special memory of a great day out with the boys."

destination ZOO

Seattle, Wa
July 2006

DESTINATION ZOO
by Alissa Fast

Album is 6 x 12"
Patterned paper: Making Memories; Chipboard:
Worldwin; Stickers: 7 Gypsies; Decorative tape,
stamps, journaling spots, alphabet masks: Heidi
Swapp; Ink: Tsukineko; Pen: Zig; Binder rings:
Office supply

Alissa used alphabet masks to create the
titles on her pages—she outlined each letter,
repositioned it, then outlined it again for a cool
dimensional look.

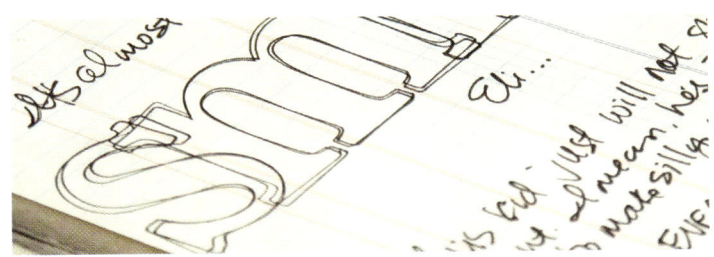

" I created this mini album to document my family's annual summer vacation to Cape Cod. We always like to go to the same places every year, so I decided to create a mini album to document all of the wonderful reasons why we love the beach. This is the only time during the year that we enjoy uninterrupted family time away from daily hectic life—computers, cell phones and work are all left at home. It really is all about family, fun, spending time with cousins, being together and enjoying each other's company. When I start a mini album, I usually find myself working on the cover last. I always have a plan for the direction of the inside, but I find more inspiration for a unique title and cover for the book after doing the journaling. I think using photos on the cover of an album is the perfect way to set the tone—in this case, I used a beautiful and relaxing picture of the ocean."

ONCE A YEAR
by Diane Ditullio

Album is 6 x 8 ½"
Cardstock: Bazzill Basics, Cactus Pink; Patterned paper, ribbon: Cactus Pink; Chipboard: Heidi Swapp, Magistical Memories; Button: Autumn Leaves, Foof-a-La; Punches: Marvy Uchida; Ink: ColorBox; Scalloped scissors: Fiskars; Pens: Uni-Ball Signo

This adorable album was created using paper from the Cactus Pink Candi and Wildflower collections. Diane uses a soft pink, brown, and blue color combination throughout, which fits with the fun and relaxed mood of the photos.

"Our sailing trips with my grandfather are very dear to me. It is precious time that I really treasure with him, and I wanted something special to capture some of our moments. I used a small journal that I could add photos to and write the memories in so that they can be remembered and shared. This little album is one of the smallest that I have, and yet it is the most precious."

SAILING JOURNAL by Jamie Harper

Album is 8 x 4 ½"
Patterned paper, charms, metal embellishments, stickers, vellum words, tag book: CR Gibson; Stamps: Heidi Swapp; Ink: StazOn; Pen: Zig

This tag book by CR Gibson is perfect for documenting a trip. Jamie uses nautical paper and embellishments to enhance the theme. Notice her creative photographs—they are all different shapes, sizes and color tones. Through her photos, design and journaling, Jamie really holds your interest as you turn the pages.

"I wanted to put together a mini album of a recent trip to Milwaukee with my boyfriend—something fast and simple to record the great time we had. Since I was short on time, I decided to use a limited amount of supplies and keep the design very simple. I was able to create this album using only one sheet of stickers, one piece of patterned paper, two pieces of cardstock, and one sheet of word stickers...all for under $10! Keeping the design uniform and easy to replicate, it only took me one afternoon to complete. I love how it turned out and my boyfriend did too!"

OUR MILWAUKEE TRIP TOGETHER by Kelly Purkey

Album is 7 ½ x 4 ¾"
Cardstock: Bazzill Basics; Patterned paper, pen: American Crafts; Stickers: American Crafts, EK Success; Stamps: Fontwerks; Ink: StazOn; Album: SEI

Kelly's album has great flow, due to its consistent page pattern and story-like journaling. She used matching cardstock and patterned paper on each page, as well as the same journaling spot stamp.

 Two years ago I decided to surprise my boyfriend, James, with a birthday trip to San Francisco. Neither of us had ever been there and we'd both been talking about how much we wanted to see the city. We had so much fun being tourists! We started at Pier 39, walked up the famous Lombard Street and visited Alcatraz, Golden Gate Park, Ghirardelli and China Town. I shouldn't forget to mention that we basically ate our way through the city…so much delicious food! We took a day trip to Monterey where I had another surprise planned for James—a behind the scenes tour of the Monterey Bay Aquarium. Unfortunately, we only had a short time in such a wonderful city. The entire trip was amazing and I knew that I had to put all of our memories in a special mini album."

SAN FRANCISCO by Mara Siegel

Album is 9 ¾ x 4 ¾"

Cardstock: Bazzill Basics; Patterned paper: Basic Grey, cherryArte, Crate Paper, Fancy Pants Designs, Hambly Studios, KI Memories, My Mind's Eye, Sassafras Lass, Scenic Route Paper Co., SEI; Wrapping paper: Paper Source; Pins: Heidi Grace Designs; Brads: Making Memories, Paper Source; Metal embellishment, bubble word: Li'l Davis Designs; Ribbon: Li'l Davis Designs, May Arts; Chipboard: Fancy Pants Designs, Heidi Swapp, Li'l Davis Designs; Flowers: American Crafts, My Mind's Eye; Buttons: Foof-a-La, Making Memories; Tag: My Mind's Eye; Rub ons: American Crafts, Li'l Davis Designs; Stickers: American Crafts, KI Memories; Ghost star: Heidi Swapp; Tab: Scrapworks; Stamps: 7 Gypsies, Autumn Leaves; Ink: StazOn; Pen: Micron; Mini album: 7 Gypsies; Circle cutter: Creative Memories; Other: Staples, ticket

Mara used wrapping paper to create a colorful cover for her mini album. Each page in the album is an envelope that could easily be used for storing memorabilia or hidden journaling.

 I took an overwhelming amount of pictures while we were on vacation to Colorado last summer. With almost 1,000 pictures, I had a lot of "extras" that I wasn't sure what to do with. I didn't want to just file them away, so I thought a mini album was definitely in order—something I could display on my coffee table with fun facts about our vacation. 'Days of the week' journaling spots by Heidi Swapp worked perfectly to document different happenings throughout the trip. I love our Colorado vacation album—I can flip through it anytime and remember that special week!"

COLORADO FAMILY VACATION

by Tina Albertson

Album is 7 ¼ x 5 ¾"
Patterned paper, silver handle, gaffer tape, stickers, card: 7 Gypsies; Deco brads, chipboard: Making Memories; Felt: American Crafts; Rub ons: 7 Gypsies, Heidi Swapp; Flowers: Bazzill Basics, Heidi Swapp, Prima; Buttons: Buttons Galore and More, Foof-a-La; Journaling spots: Heidi Swapp; Stamps: 7 Gypsies, Autumn Leaves; Ink: ColorBox; Scalloped scissors: EK Success; Pen: Zig

Combine writing styles in your albums. Tina mixes it up with a conversation she had with her daughter, feelings about the trip from her point of view, and on the last page she uses day stickers to write about what they did on each day.

 As my children have gotten older, I like to reflect back on the day we first met—when they were innocent little bundles. My heart was so full of humility and awe at the wonder of their recent birth, the miracle of life and the blessing of my children. It's also fun for the kids to compare their birth statistics and to see themselves as little babies. This book gets a lot of use at our house! Converting the photos to black and white helped cover for the not-so-great camera I had when my first son was born, and also helped unify the album."

Album is 7 ¼ x 6 ½"
Cardstock: Prism; Patterned paper, binder, flowers, stickers: Bo-Bunny Press; Eyelets, brads: Karen Foster Design; Charms: All My Memories, Karen Foster Design; Metal hinge: Making Memories; Ribbon: Bo-Bunny Press, Offray, Scrapworks; Chipboard: Heidi Swapp; Tags: 7 Gypsies, Making Memories (metal-rimmed); Rub ons: Bo-Bunny Press, KI Memories; Ink: ColorBox; Square punch: Marvy Uchida; Pens: Sharpie, Zig; Other: Safety pin

For a dressed up (and gender-neutral) album, Shaunte paired black & white photos with coordinating black, white and cream album, paper, and embellishments. For her twin page, she stacked "IT'S A BOY" and "IT'S A GIRL" tags and attached them to the page with a hinge so you can lift it to see more writing underneath.

IT'S A BOY!

INSTRUCTIONS:
SPOIL ROTTEN, SHOW UNCONDITIONAL LOVE, GIVE WET KISSES CONTINUALLY.

FORM - [ID2.444#056#]

NAME	Brendan Taylor		baby
DATE	2-12-98	TIME 9:32 a.m.	
WEIGHT	7lb 14oz	LENGTH 20"	No. 2
EYES	Blue	HAIR Brown	
HOME			

PARENTS PLEASE FILL IN WITH LOVE AND CARE

XOXOXO

IT'S A BOY!
IT'S A GIRL!

INSTRUCTIONS:
SPOIL ROTTEN, SHOW UNCONDITIONAL LOVE, GIVE WET KISSES CONTINUALLY.

FORM - [ID2.444#056#]

NAME	Shianne		baby
DATE	8-5-99	TIME 7:13 p.m.	
WEIGHT	4lb 5oz	LENGTH 17½"	No. 3
EYES	Blue	HAIR little	
HOME			

PARENTS PLEASE FILL IN WITH LOVE AND CARE

IT'S A GIRL!

NAME Mikayla
DATE 4-21-03   TIME 8:57 a.m.   baby
WEIGHT 7lb 12oz   LENGTH 18½"   No. 5
EYES Blue   HAIR Black
HOME

> "With my daughter growing and changing every day, it is difficult to document each special moment with its own layout. I decided to create this little book to make sure that I didn't miss those daily memories that sometimes get forgotten. I planned it the same way I would plan out a layout, arranging photos and choosing papers and embellishments that would complement them. I know my family and I will cherish this book for years to come because of the memories it holds and because of its unique shape and style."

SARAH @ 2 by Alexis Hardy

Album is 3" across

Cardstock: Bazzill Basics; Patterned paper: Basic Grey, Hambly Studios, Urban Lily; Brads: Creative Imaginations, Making Memories; Ribbon: Michaels; Chipboard: Bazzill Basics, Technique Tuesday, Urban Lily; Flowers: Doodlebug Design, Making Memories, Michaels; Buttons: Autumn Leaves, Doodlebug Design; Tags: Making Memories; Die cuts: Doodlebug Design, My Mind's Eye; Rub ons: 7 Gypsies, Basic Grey, Hambly Studios, Urban Lily; Stickers: 7 Gypsies, American Crafts, Creative Imaginations, Heidi Swapp, Making Memories, Sticko, Urban Lily; Stamps: Poppy Ink, Stampin' Up!, Technique Tuesday; Ink: Tsukineko; Pens: Marvy Uchida, Uni-Ball Signo, Zig; Jewels: me & my BIG ideas, DM Productions; Overlays: Hambly Studios; Plastic butterfly: Autumn Leaves

Alexis enhances the girly theme in this little album with girly embellishments—rub on wings, a crown, flowers and jewels.

" This mini album is very special to me because it contains baby photos from all of the women in my family, from my great-grandmother down to my daughter. I created this album for my daughter so that important information about her ancestors will not be lost, and so she can get to know a little about her grandmothers who have passed on. It is also fun to look through the photos and pick out some family resemblances! To give the album a uniform feel, I scanned the heritage photos and cropped them to the same size and format, then adjusted the hue and saturation."

GENERATIONS by Betsy Veldman

Album is 5" across

Cardstock: Bazzill Basics; Patterned paper: A2Z Essentials, Scenic Route Paper Co.; Brads: Paper Studio; Ribbon: Creative Imaginations, unknown; Stickers: Crafty Secrets, EK Success; Stamps: Purple Onion Designs; Ink: Ranger; Clock face, hands, and Roman numerals: Craft supply

What a fun and unique way to display your family tree! When doing a lot of sewing, make sure to do the stitching before adhering the pages together so it doesn't show on the other side.

FoRever my baby

Be Inspired

- no matter how big you get.

"This book is actually a gift album. The inside pages are blank and the covers are covered with photos and blue colors. The photo tabs are my favorite part—they really add to the style and feel of this album. It's a perfect gift for a new mom!"

BABY BOARD BOOK by Jamie Harper

Album is 6 ¾ x 6 ¼"
Cardstock: Bazzill Basics; Patterned paper, rub ons: Carolee's Creations; Pen: Zig

To make these photo tabs, Jamie simply cut eight photos to 1 x 2", rounded the corners and glued them back-to-back with a page edge sandwiched in between. Make sure when cropping pictures that you can still clearly tell what the picture is of.

BABY

My favorite gift to give to new parents is a photo shoot. Our good friends Josh and Marcie welcomed sweet little Addison into their family in October, and these are some of the pictures I took. I wanted to keep the album simple and keep the focus on the pictures, so I kept embellishments to a minimum. I thought that the Wild Asparagus paper provided just the right girly touch without overwhelming the photos."

ADDISON'S ALBUM

by Valerie Laramee

Album is 9 ½ x 6 ½"
Cardstock: Bazzill Basics; Patterned paper: My Mind's Eye; Brads: Die Cuts with a View, Making Memories; Ribbon: Offray; Chipboard, ghost hearts, flower jewel: Heidi Swapp; Flowers: Prima; Rub ons: Heidi Swapp, Making Memories; Stickers: 7 Gypsies, Making Memories, Pebbles, Inc.; Font: Jiffy, from myfonts.com; Album: American Crafts

Valerie generated fluidity and uniformity in her album by using consistent colors and patterned paper throughout.

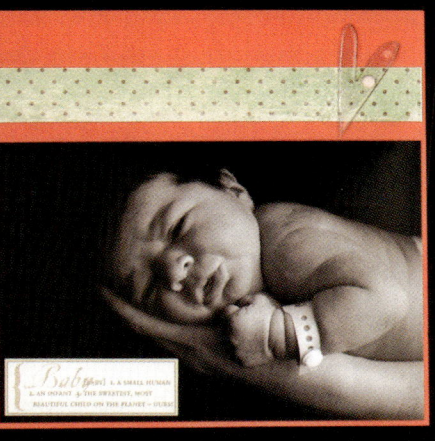

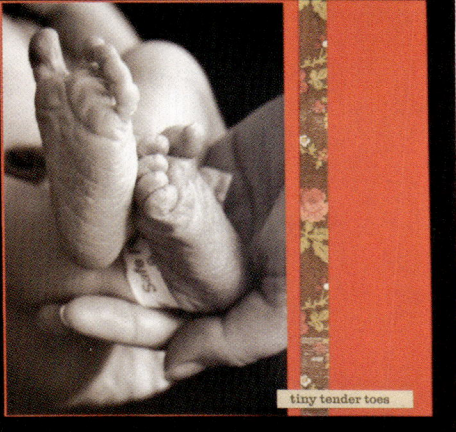

 This album holds a special place in my heart since it is devoted to my family. It tells what each one contributes to our household, and how together we make one colorful group! We all have our own distinct personalities and quirks, so making this album was a lot of fun."

OUR COLORFUL FAMILY
by Tina Albertson

Album is 8" square
Cardstock: Bazzill Basics, KI Memories; Patterned paper, ribbon, tags, stickers: KI Memories; Brads: Bazzill Basics, Making Memories; Staples: Making Memories; Chipboard: Basic Grey, Heidi Swapp, KI Memories, Making Memories; Flowers: Heidi Swapp, Making Memories, Prima; Acrylic: Heidi Swapp, KI Memories; Buttons: Doodlebug Design, Foof-a-La; Rub ons: Color Theory, KI Memories; Ink: ColorBox; Paint: Heidi Swapp, Li'l Davis Designs; Pen: Zig; Journaling Spots: Heidi Swapp

In keeping with the "colorful family" theme, Tina used color to great effect in her album. Each family member's page is in shades of the color that matches their personality. To make the "colorful" flower on the cover, Tina placed KI Memories letter stickers in a circle on cardstock, then cut out around each one, added a sticker in the center and a stem and leaves beneath. The chipboard letters ("our") were painted with Heidi Swapp paint, then coated with glitter glaze.

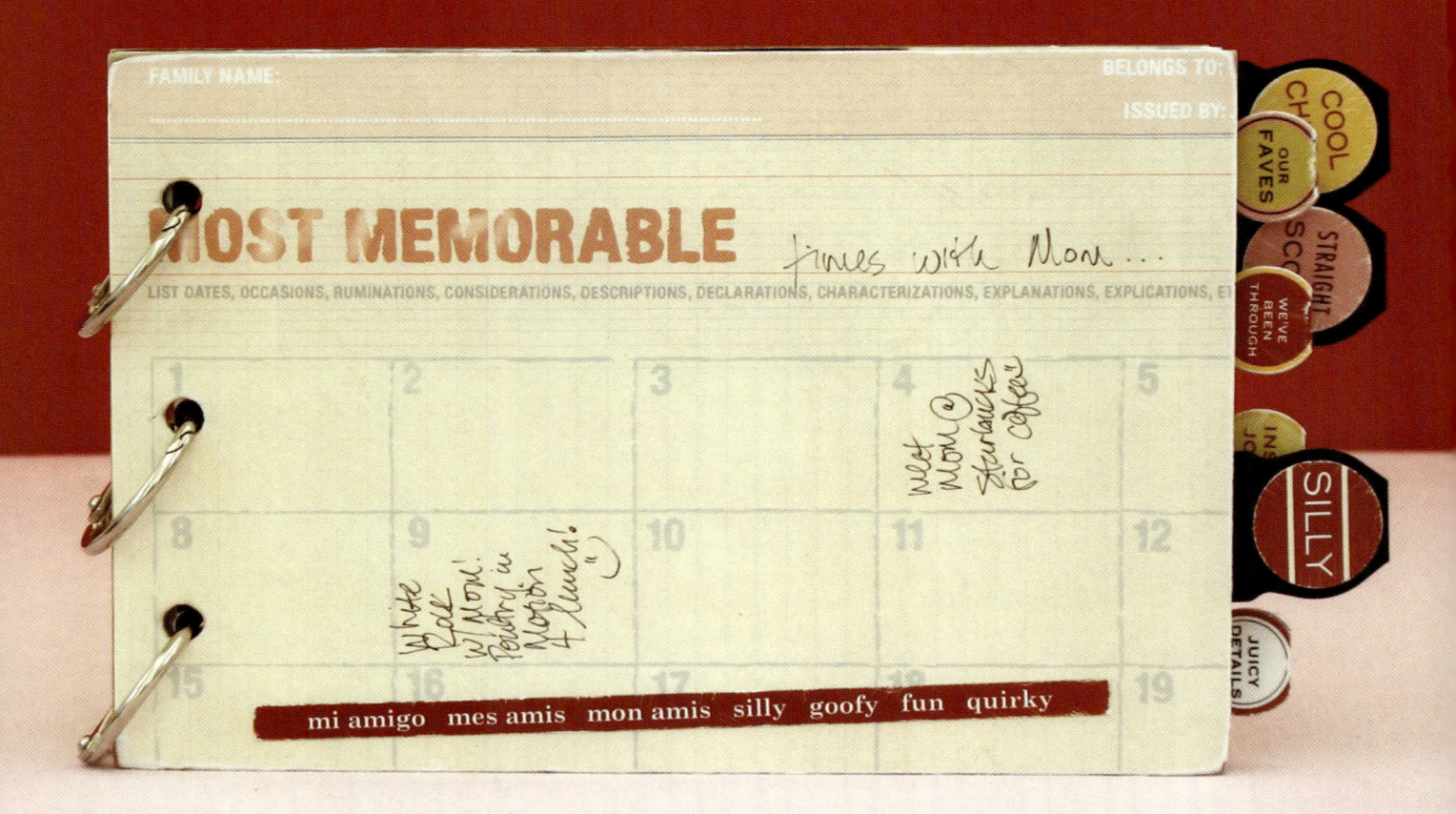

"My mom and I spend a lot of time together—we love to go places to take photos, have lunch, shop, and we especially love to go to Starbucks. This calendar paper from 7 Gypsies was my inspiration for the album's theme; I thought it would be a great place to house some of my favorite photos of times with Mom. The 7 Gypsies album pages are just bigger than 5 x 7", so they're perfect for 5 x 7" photos."

MOST MEMORABLE TIMES WITH MOM by Alissa Fast

Album is 7 ½ x 5" Patterned paper, metal embellishments, stickers, binder ring album, journaling tags: 7 Gypsies; Pens: American Crafts, Sharpie

Notice Alyssa's use of patterned paper: She cut two big lines of scallops down the sides of patterned paper blocks (that were the same size as her album pages), then adhered the left and right pieces to the left and right edges of another page. She adhered the middle piece to its own page, creating the same effect. Check out 7gypsies.com for great mini album products like the journaling tags Alissa used.

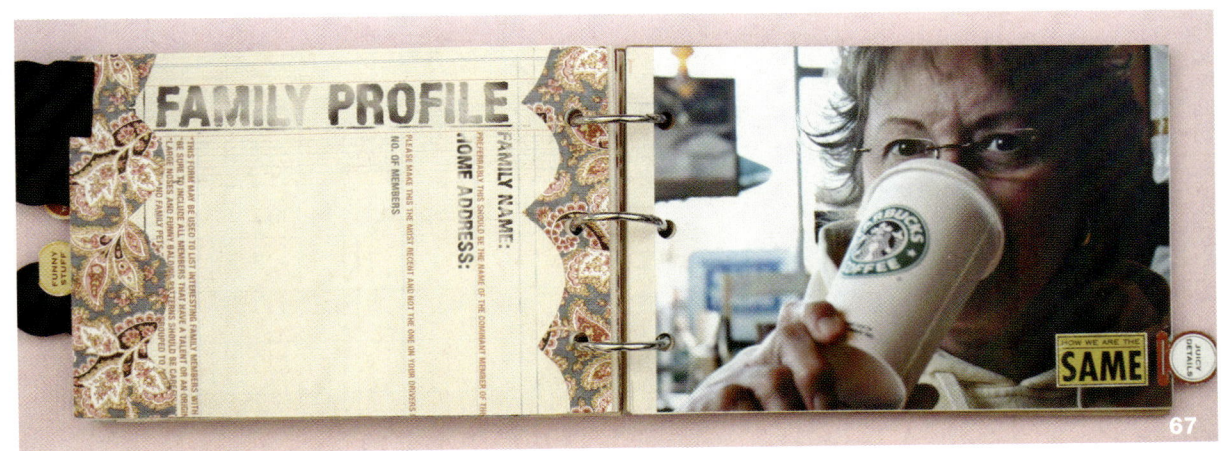

 My two year old son calls us the cuddlin' and kissin' family—and it's true! With this in mind, I wanted to create an album that celebrated our family's affectionate nature. The album really began with our 'mission statement' which I printed and used as the back cover. It says: 'Hafermann Family Mission Statement: We are in the business of love and support. We believe in displaying affection; showing our love and appreciation. We value hugs and kind words. We aim to make life richer and fuller for those we care about.' I gathered pictures that fit this theme, then used a one-picture-per-page scheme, adding a fun quote about love and affection to each page. I chose to use a sturdy board book so my son can easily handle it."

SWAK by Anne Hafermann

We are a kissin', huggin', fun-lovin' kind of family. Sappy, tender, & affectionate – just the way we like it!

Any man who can drive safely while kissing a pretty girl is simply not giving the kiss the attention it deserves.

~Albert Einstein

Hugs & kisses, warmth & caring,
Parent and child, their hearts as one–
A link that can never be undone.

Album is 4" square

Patterned paper: 7 Gypsies, KI Memories; Charms: American Crafts, craft supply; Ribbon: Craft supply, Offray; Chipboard: Maya Road; Flowers: 7 Gypsies, American Crafts, Craft supply; Rub ons, sequins: Doodlebug Design; Crystals: Making Memories; Stickers: American Crafts; Stamps, ink: Impress; Font: Typical Writer, from simplythebest.net/fonts

Anne mixed her own cute custom flowers with pre-made ones. To make your own, simply punch a circle from patterned paper or cardstock and snip small triangles from the edges. Turn up the petals for some dimension.

 I am an 8 ½ x 11" scrapbooker—period. However, I do love a good challenge, so in response to a challenge from my friends, I created this book. I wanted to make something for my family that shows us for who we are and what we love. I came up with a collage of photos from a very special day underneath the inside flaps, and it makes me so happy just to look at it."

Album is 5 x 6 ½"

Cardstock: Bazzill Basics; Patterned paper: Scenic Route Paper Co.; Ribbon, mini portfolio album kit: 7 Gypsies; Chipboard, flowers: Heidi Swapp; Rub ons, stickers: American Crafts; Font: Babel Sans, from dafont.com

Courtney arranged her pictures digitally before printing them on one sheet. She printed her journaling on cardstock strips that she adhered to cream cardstock; the cardstock is adhered beneath the photo collage and folded over to create two flaps.

 I created this book to be an ongoing record of things we have done in our home through the years—not only the physical improvements, but our family life as well. I view it as an 'if these walls could talk' story! I started with a photo of the house, and then added a recent family photo and a family quote to focus on what really makes this house a home. I included our pets since they are such an important part of our family."

H IS FOR HOME by Carolyn Lontin

Album is 6 x 7"

Album, cardstock, patterned paper, photo anchors, stickers: 7 Gypsies; Brads: Die Cuts with a View; Bone clip: Creative Imaginations; Chipboard: Making Memories, Heidi Swapp; Buttons: Making Memories; Rub ons: 7 Gypsies, Chatterbox, Junkitz, Phrase Café; Stamps: Technique Tuesday; Ink: Memories Complete

 My husband and I often comment on how amazingly well our daughters get along. They play together so well and genuinely love to be together. They are 5 and 2 years old, and even with a 3 year age difference, they are inseparable. I have tons of photos of them together and thought it would be fun to make a 'sisters' album about their special relationship. I used hand journaling (not an easy thing for me) because I wanted it to be personal and special for the girls. I hope it will be something they will cherish for years to come."

SISTERS by Maria Burke

Album is 7 ½ x 6 ½" Cardstock, iron ons, flowers, stickers: SEI; Patterned paper: 7 Gypsies, Scenic Route Paper Co., SEI; Corner rounder: All Night Media; Stamps: Autumn Leaves; Ink: StazOn; Pen: Office supply; Album: Pioneer

Maria chose to use soft pretty pinks and blues; the velvet iron ons on the cover and the rounded corners throughout add to the softness of the album.

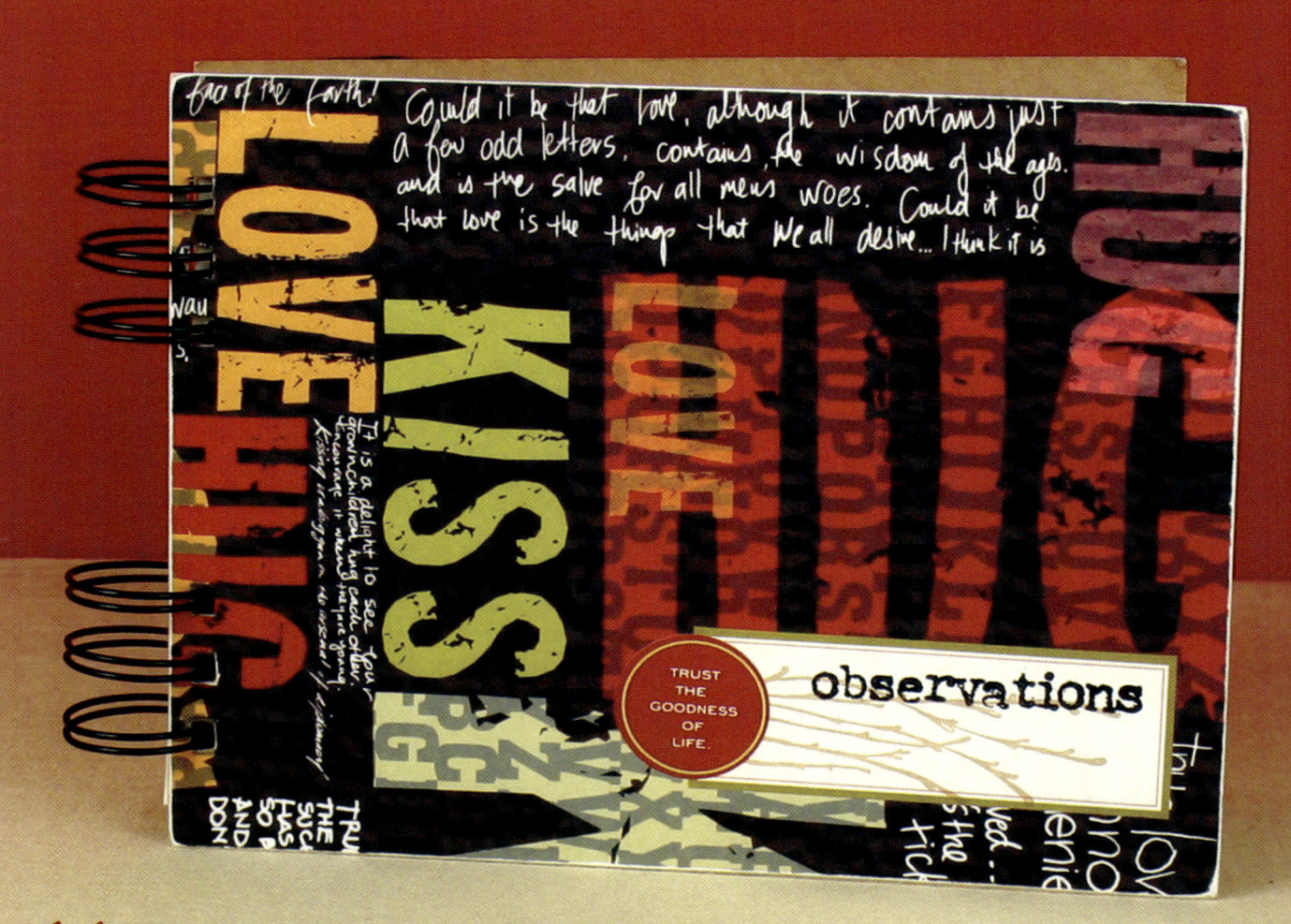

> This album was made from a 7 Gypsies recipe album kit, but I decided I would use the three tabs to document my husband and two daughters throughout the year instead. I covered the tabs with paper, then added some journaling lines and a square photo of the subject to each of the tabbed pages. Using coordinating stickers and patterned paper made it easy. I keep this album in the kitchen to remind me to snap frequent photos and make notes about the funny things my family does throughout the year."

OBSERVATIONS by Marci Lambert

Album is 7 x 5 ¾"
Patterned paper, stickers, gaffer tape, mini album: 7 Gypsies;
Corner rounder: EK Success; Stamps: Technique Tuesday, Posh
Impressions; Ink: ColorBox, Tsukineko; Pen: Pilot

This album has a great design that would be simple to
recreate. Cover part of the pages with patterned paper,
round the corners of your photographs and adhere.
Attach labels on the tabs and embellish with 7 Gypsies
stickers and gaffer tape. Leave empty pages to fill in later.

 "This album is just for me—I wanted to have a place just to show why I create. My family means the world to me, so I recorded why I love them so much and the many ways I am inspired by them. I used vivid and fun colors to keep the feeling very alive and bright."

CRE-8 A LIFE THAT YOU LOVE by Jamie Harper

Album is 9 x 8"
Cardstock: Bazzill Basics; Patterned paper: Autumn Leaves, Crate Paper, Foof-a-La, Making Memories, Scenic Route Paper Co.; Brads: Bazzill Basics; Fabric: Jo-Ann Scrap Essentials; Ribbon: 7 Gypsies, Carolee's Creations; Chipboard: Maya Road (flowers), Scenic Route Paper Co. (letters); Flowers, chipboard book: Maya Road; Tags: Heidi Swapp; Rub ons: Scenic Route Paper Co.; Stickers: Carolee's Creations, Scenic Route Paper Co.; Decorative tape: Heidi Swapp; Pen: Zig; Rhinestones: me & my BIG ideas; Photography: Jamie Harper, Suzy Plantamura

Jamie uses a lot of visually interesting elements in her album. She combined black & white and color photos for variety and even enlarged one photograph to fill an entire page. Notice her variety of tabs, using fabric, ribbon, stickers, and decorative paper clips. Very creative!

 The lyrics on the inside of the accordion album are to a song my mother sang to me when I was little and now I sing it to my daughter. After I finished the album, I gave it to my daughter to keep in her room and look at whenever she wanted. She loves it—in fact, she was sad when I told her I was sending it away to be published! I can't wait to see her little face when I give it back to her."

I ♡ U by Amanda Johnston

Album is 2 x 2 ¼"
Cardstock: Crafts, Etc.; Patterned paper: Anna Griffin, Inc.; Flowers: Prima; Rub ons: Daisy Hill, Gin-X; Tin: Dongguan City Wanxinlong Metal Manufacture Co., Ltd.; Gems: Puttin' on the Glitz; Diamond glaze: JudiKins; Pen: Pigment Pro; Font: Century Gothic

Amanda used clear liquid adhesive to glue the gems and Prima flower in place. She printed the pictures from her computer using the index print feature; they came out just the right size.

 I made this garland as a fun project to hang in my studio each year for Valentine's Day...or all year 'roun[d]
It's so much fun to have photos of my three loves hanging around."

LOVE GARLAND by Keisha Campbell

Album is 6" square
Patterned paper: 7 Gypsies, Making Memories; Charm: Unknown; Metal clips: Li'l Davis Designs; Chipboard: Heidi Swapp, Jenni Bowlin Studios, Pressed Petals; Acrylic letters: Making Memories; Buttons: Jenni Bowlin Studios; Stickers: Heidi Swapp; Stamps: Autumn Leaves; Ink: StazOn;

This chipboard love garland is a beautiful mini album for your family to look through and be reminded how special they are to you. It can easily be hung up in your house for them to see every day.

 The age of twelve is often a difficult time for young girls, and Ansley is no exception. I created this mini album using a random collection of some of my favorite photos of her because I wanted her to see through my eyes what a wonderful person she is. I want her to realize that she walks with grace and carries herself with style without even trying. I want her to know that she has what it takes to make it in this world and achieve her dreams. Most importantly, whenever Ansley doubts herself, I hope she will reflect upon this mini album and remember that she is my superstar, and that I know she will go far."

U R MY SUPERSTAR by Lisa M. Pace

Album is 3 x 4 ½"
Patterned paper: Scenic Route Paper Co.; Floss: DMC; Ribbon: Offray; Buttons: Unknown; Rhinestones: Darice; Glitter: Art Institute; Rub ons, ghost letters, chipboard, photo corners, mask: Heidi Swapp; Clear tabs: Office supply; Paint: Making Memories; Font: Times New Roman; Other: Staples

Lisa attached plastic over her pictures to protect them and give them a cool glossy look; she adhered her journaling over the top. For a decorative touch on the back, she adhered a line of pre-sewn buttons over the path of the ribbon.

 It is not always easy to find willing participants for photo shoots around my home, so when my daughter Taylor volunteered, I couldn't let the rare opportunity pass me by. After our impromptu session I was eager to proof the photos, but to my surprise, I didn't see my little girl anymore! I saw a beautiful young lady who was growing up before my very eyes. I wanted to celebrate my daughter becoming a young lady, so blooming flowers seemed the perfect way to accent her photos."

SHE'S BLOOMING INTO A YOUNG LADY by Susan Tutt

I love the pictures from our little photo shoot. These pictures truly capture your personality. I love you, my sweet girl. October 2006.

Taylor you are 11 years old and changing in so many ways. You are becoming a young lady right before our very eyes. One thing that hasn't changed is how sweet you are, and I hope it never does.

Album is 6 ½ x 4 ½"
Cardstock: Die Cuts with a View; Patterned paper, buttons: Autumn Leaves; Vellum: Unknown; Chipboard, tin: Maya Road; Stickers, paint: Making Memories; Decorative tape: 7 Gypsies; Stamps: Autumn Leaves, Maya Road; Ink: Tsukineko; Font: CK Elsie

When stamping on fabric, Susan always applies a layer of decoupage to the fabric and lets it dry before stamping. This gives the fabric more body and pliability, which is particularly important if you're cutting out the image, as she did with some of the flowers.

TrendSetters

Fifteen top scrapbookers. One amazing book.

scrapbook
TRENDS

GET UP CLOSE AND PERSONAL with some of the industry's hottest scrapbookers! As these women have moved to the forefront of the industry over the past few years, they have been featured in multiple publications, won a myriad of contests, created countless designs for top scrapbooking companies and also occupy positions on many design teams. But more than that, their fresh ideas, amazing creations and meaningful journaling caught our eye — they are true trendsetters as they provide inspiration to scrappers everywhere. Sneak a peek into their lives and see what inspires them as they share their favorite tips and tricks. With mini albums, cards, layouts and more, not only will they give you lots of fun ideas, but you will feel like you have several new friends. Come see why we have named these 15 ladies the Scrapbook "TrendSetters" class of 2006!

Make your own mini album

by Paige Taylor

I LOVE MINI ALBUMS. What more can I say? There's nothing quite like the look on someone's face when you hand them a little book you poured your heart and soul into. Some mini albums take only a few minutes to make and assemble, while others take months—possibly even years—to completely finish, as you continue to add to and perfect them.

During my time at Scrapbook Trends, I have seen some amazing albums come through our offices. I've often asked myself, "How did she do that? Did she make that herself?" With a little help from online sources and shared knowledge from expert bookbinders, I've come up with three easy mini albums that you can make *yourself* from the ground up. Here's to ongoing mini album inspiration!

Accordian Album

The most popular type of mini album I see submitted to us for publication is definitely the accordion album. Accordion albums are wonderful because they're easy to make and are a fun way to display your favorite photos, whether you keep the book folded for occasional viewing or open on a shelf.

CREATIVE ALTERNATIVES:

· Stitch blocks of cardstock or patterned paper to the bottom of your inner pages to create pockets for storing extra pictures or memorabilia.

· Use ribbon to keep your book closed: Glue the ends of two pieces of ribbon inside the covers and tie in a bow, wrap an extra-long length around the album several times before tying it closed, or simply knot it around once for a pretty finishing touch.

DIRECTIONS:

1) First, decide the size of your mini album when it's closed. I will make a 3" square album for this example.

2) Next, choose the material for your inner pages. Patterned cardstock and tagboard seem to work best but you could make thick fabric or even extra-wide ribbon work as well.

3) Trim your material to the same height as your album. In this case, I will cut 3" tall strips from tagboard. 3" and 4" heights are the most convenient, because you can get an even number from a standard 12 x 12" sheet. For example, I can get four blocks of 3" tall pieces from my 12 x 12" sheet of tagboard (each block is 12 x 3").

4) Score each block the same number of inches as the width of your album. Since I want my album to be 3" square, I will score every 3".

5) Adhere the last sections on the strips together until you have the number of pages you want. Fold your long block of material accordion style on the scored lines.

6) Next, make the covers. Cut two blocks of tagboard, cardboard, chipboard, or any other hard material—such as Plexiglas®, old CDs, etc.—to the same size of your album, or slightly larger.

7) Adhere the front cover to the first page and the back cover to the last page.

8) Embellish your pages with paper, pictures, ribbon, journaling and more. This makes a great brag book!

Single Sheet Binding

Are you tired of all those holiday and birthday cards, wedding invitations and baby announcements cluttering up your drawers? Take them from mess to mini album in just an evening. You could also throw postcards, letters, pictures and other memorabilia into the mix for a book that's totally personal and totally unique.

YOU WILL NEED:

TAGBOARD, CARDBOARD, PATTERNED PAPER, FABRIC, CARDS (basically anything will work for the pages)

BINDER RINGS, RIBBON, THREAD, STRING, TWIST-TIES, PAPER CLIPS, ETC. (for the binding)

HOLE PUNCH (plain or shaped)

SPECIALTY SCISSORS (optional)

CREATIVE ALTERNATIVES:

· Instead of punching holes down the left side, align all your items at the top left corner and punch a hole there. Fasten together with a binder ring, ribbon, or twist-tie.

· Tie it all together with a pretty cover. Cut two blocks of chipboard just larger than your largest inner page, embellish them with patterned paper and sandwich everything inside.

DIRECTIONS:

1) First, decide what you want your mini album to be made up of. For this example, I am using random cards and invitations that I have stored for years. You could also use pre-made pages (in or out of page protectors), leftover pictures without a home, postcards, tickets, travel itineraries, receipts, and other paraphernalia you're ready to scrap.

2) Next, decide if you want your pages to be the same or different sizes. Trim your pages if you want them uniform; I like the look of different sizes and will simply use my cards "as is" for the mini album base.

3) Align all your items so the left edges are flush.

4) Punch holes down the left edge. Use a 3-hole punch if your items are large enough (you could use just two of the three holes if they're smaller), or use a hand punch. For a decorative look, use a shaped hole punch such as a heart, star, oval or square.

5) Bind the book together via the holes you've punched; here are several options:
   - Metal binder rings *(great if you want to add more pages later)*
   - Ribbon *(all the same, or mix it up with different colors, textures and lengths)*
   - Twist ties *(again, easy to undo and add more pages)*
   - Large paper clips or wire
   - Lace it like a shoe using twine, string, ribbon or shoelaces

6) Adorn each page to your heart's content and you have a fabulous album!

Tagboard Album

This album is just like the kind you might buy from a store, only it's tailored to your specific needs (and cheaper, if you don't mind putting a little work into it). And it comes together in 8 easy steps, so you can make several of these while sitting in front of the television watching your favorite shows.

CREATIVE ALTERNATIVES:

· After you've adhered the pages together, try cutting the entire book into a unique shape, such as an oval, heart or star. Just be sure to leave a generous portion of the spine intact.

· Make an interactive baby book using fabric for your pages. A little quilt batting will make it soft and pretty hand stitching can keep the batting in place. (You could even print your favorite photos on cloth!)

1) After choosing a size (mine is 6" square), gather the material for your album. Tagboard/chipboard, cardboard, cardstock and patterned paper are excellent choices. I will use tagboard for this album. (Ask your local scrapbook store for extra sheets of this sturdy material—it comes at the bottom of packs of patterned paper—or search for it online).

2) Next, cut the sheets for your inside pages. To get the right dimensions, double the width of your album and keep the height the same. Since my finished book will be 6 x 6", I need to cut the tagboard to 12 x 6".

3) Cut as many sheets as you want inside spreads. If you want five spreads (10 pages), you need to cut five sheets of material; take into account the front and back covers. If you're using a sturdy enough material, the back of the first spread can double as the front cover.

4) Score down the middle of each sheet (in this case at the 6" mark), and fold in half. Stack your folded sheets together with the folded edge on the left side, just like the actual book will be in the end.

5) Adhere the backs of your sheets together using a strong adhesive. Place something heavy on top when you're done to help the adhesive bond.

6) If your pages are uneven, you can take the stack to Kinko's or another copy center and pay a small fee to have the edges trimmed. You could also sand the edges until they are flush, or leave them as is—after all, little imperfections make a mini album unique. If you've got heavy-duty specialty scissors, you could even scallop the edges.

7) Next it's time to make the cover. If you've used something sturdy for the pages, you can simply cover the spine with fabric tape (7 Gypsies and Making Memories both offer decorative options) and call it good. Or you can cut a separate piece of tagboard for the covers, taking into account a little extra length for the spine, and glue the first and last pages to it.

8) Have fun decorating and embellishing your "from scratch" mini album!

With the same beautiful photography as the outstanding CARDS Idea Book Series, the improved Scrapbook Trends has a fabulous new look *plus* 32 more pages! That's 164 pages of the creative layouts you love, along with fun articles, mini albums and cards, all packaged in a fun new size. Get ready for Scrapbook Trends to inspire you more than ever—grab your copy today!

Call 1.888.225.9199 or order online at scrapbooktrendsmag.com

scrapbook TRENDS

Your Layouts

Your Projects

YOUR BOOK

 Throughout my life, I have had many reasons to shed tears, for both happy and sad events. From the birth of my children to the loss of my dear friend and grandfather, this book is a tribute to those days."

TEARS FROM SADNESS TO JOY – MY JOURNEY
by Kelly Anne Grundhauser

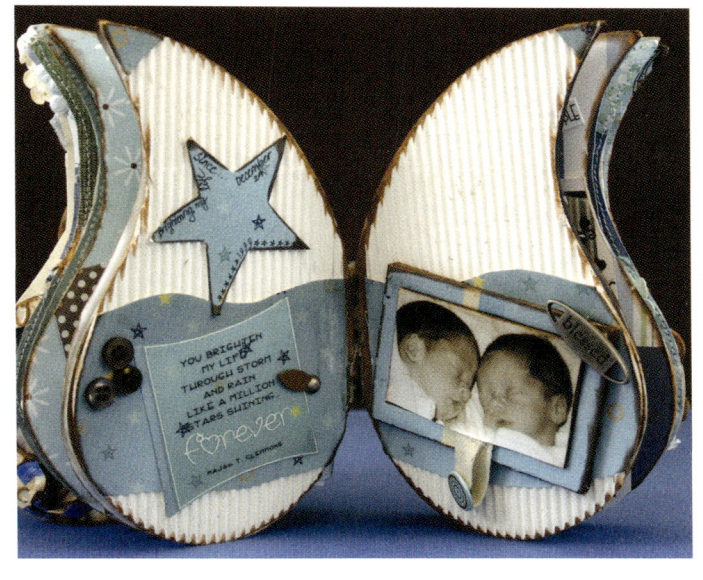

Album is 4 x 6 ½"

Cardstock: Bazzill Basics, ColorMates, Prism, The Paper Company; Patterned paper: Carolee's Creations, Chatterbox, cherryArte, Daisy D's, Flair Designs, Paper Salon, Sassafras Lass, Sweetwater, We R Memory Keepers; Brads: Accent Depot, Jo-Ann Scrap Essentials, Queen & Co.; Charms: Maya Road, unknown; Metal embellishments: K & Company ("Life's Journey" snap), Maya Road (frames), Making Memories (letters), Queen & Co. (photo turns); Ribbon: Creative Imaginations, Maya Road; Chipboard: Maya Road; Flowers: Prima; Acrylic flower: Thrift store; Buttons: Foof-a-La; Tags, paint: Heidi Swapp; Rub ons: 7 Gypsies, Chatterbox, Marcella by Kay; Stickers: EK Success, Making Memories, SEI; Stamps, ink: Paper Salon; Fluid chalk: Clearsnap; Pens: American Crafts, Sharpie, Tombo; Distressing tool: Around the Block; Clipboard: Rob and Bob Studios; Other: Bottle cap, ribbon slides, key, ribbon locket, hair bobbin

Kelly Anne's teardrop-shaped, emotion-filled album about the significance of her tears is packed full of interesting elements and creative journaling. On one page, she printed a close-up of her eyes on fabric and hid a strip of journaling behind with a flower as a pull tab. Other hidden journaling includes a picture flap with journaling on the back kept closed with a photo turn, an envelope closed with a bobby pin, and a picture on a chipboard rectangle that pulls out of a chipboard frame to reveal accordion style paper.

 This album means a lot to me because it represents the hundreds of times we've been to the beach. This day was totally unplanned—we had no intention of going to the beach, but couldn't resist when we found ourselves at my mom's house nearby. We didn't even have our swimsuits with us, but nonetheless, it was a perfect day and we ended up spending the entire afternoon there. I wanted to create a fun album and decided to make it a puzzle so my children would have as much fun playing with it as they did playing at the beach that day.

BEACH RETREAT by Hilary Kanwischer

Box is 7 x 5", puzzle is 12" square
Cardstock: Bazzill Basics; Patterned paper: Fancy Pants Designs; Brads: American Tag; Ribbon: Self-Addressed; Chipboard: Basic Grey; Flowers: Jenni Bowlin Studios; Clock face: Heidi Swapp; Tags: Daisy D's; Rub ons: Fancy Pants Designs, Li'l Davis Designs, Making Memories; Stickers: Basic Grey, Creative Imaginations; Stamps: Close To My Heart; Ink: Clearsnap, Close To My Heart; Pen: Zig; Font: Book Antiqua; Lunch pail, puzzle pieces: Creative Imaginations; Shells: Michaels; Other: Mod Podge, sandpaper

Hilary displays her memories one puzzle piece at a time. She used decoupage to cover each piece with a photograph or patterned paper, trimmed the excess and sanded the edges for a soft look and feel. Sepia photographs paired with muted colors offer a sense of relaxation and calmness that fit with the serene beach scene. When pieces are separated they fit perfectly inside her "Beach Retreat" tin.

JOY & HAPPINESS

sneaks in through a door

you didn't know you left open.

" I came home one night after a long day and as I opened my front door, I realized how happy I was to just be opening my own door. And in that moment, I thought about all the other doors in my home that I open on a daily basis that go unnoticed. Each one serves a different purpose and all of them fill me with joy. I knew I had to create a mini album about the doors in my home and the happiness they bring me."

DOOR TO MY HEART by Jami Mayes

Album is 4 ½ x 10"
Cardstock: Bazzill Basics; Ribbon: Unknown; Chipboard: K & Company; Stickers: EK Success, Heidi Swapp; Door hanger: Creative Imaginations; Font: Times New Roman

Jami wanted the photographs to take center stage and tell this story, so the album is focused on pictures more than journaling. She altered two door hangers to create the binding/cover, and glued her photos to six 4½ x 6½" rectangles for the inside pages. The pages are attached to the hangers with ribbon tied through punched holes. The inside of the back door hanger is completely covered with a photograph of a hand about to open Jami's door, which makes a cool backdrop for the other pages.

 "One afternoon when Ansley was supposed to be learning a new piece for her clarinet, she decided that trying to fly would be more interesting. After she practiced jumping and flying for a while, she felt that her new skill was ready for me to see. As I laughed and watched her jump with joy, I was reminded of stories about my Dad's fascination with flight. When he was around her age, Dad jumped off the garage roof holding an umbrella, and from the top of a hay loft with homemade wings constructed from bamboo and paper. (I'm thankful that Ansley was content to try her flying while she was still on the ground.) It occurred to me that a flipbook mini album would be a great way to document Ansley's new accomplishment and I incorporated Dad's flying stories into the journaling."

FLY by Lisa M. Pace

Paw Paw had planned for a padded landing in the hay wagon but missed his landing hit the edge of the wagon and rolled off onto the ground. His hopes of flying were dashed once again in just a few seconds.

You were supposed to be practicing your clarinet but instead decided to see if you could fly... yes, **FLY!** This flipbook is the closest I could do in helping you achieve your goal of **flying** without the means of an aircraft, spacecraft or wings!

Album is 8 x 4"
Patterned paper, rub ons: SEI; Ribbon: Basic Grey, unknown; Floss: DMC; Chipboard: Making Memories; Flowers: Doodlebug Design, Heidi Swapp, Michael Miller; Wire: Darice; Buttons: Foof-a-La, unknown; Stickles: Ranger; Ink: ColorBox; Font: Times New Roman

Lisa created the template for the butterflies in her album herself! Notice her attention to detail with the wire antennae, bead and button heads, and bodies. The butterflies on the cover have bent up wings indicating flight.

 This little album was something I made for my son and daughter to play with. It's very interactive so they can open the doors, lift the hood and simply enjoy it. They are too young to read, so this album gets them to slow down and take their time looking through a book. They really love the wheels on the front of the album and 'drive' it all over the tables at home."

THINGS THAT GO
by Kimber McGray

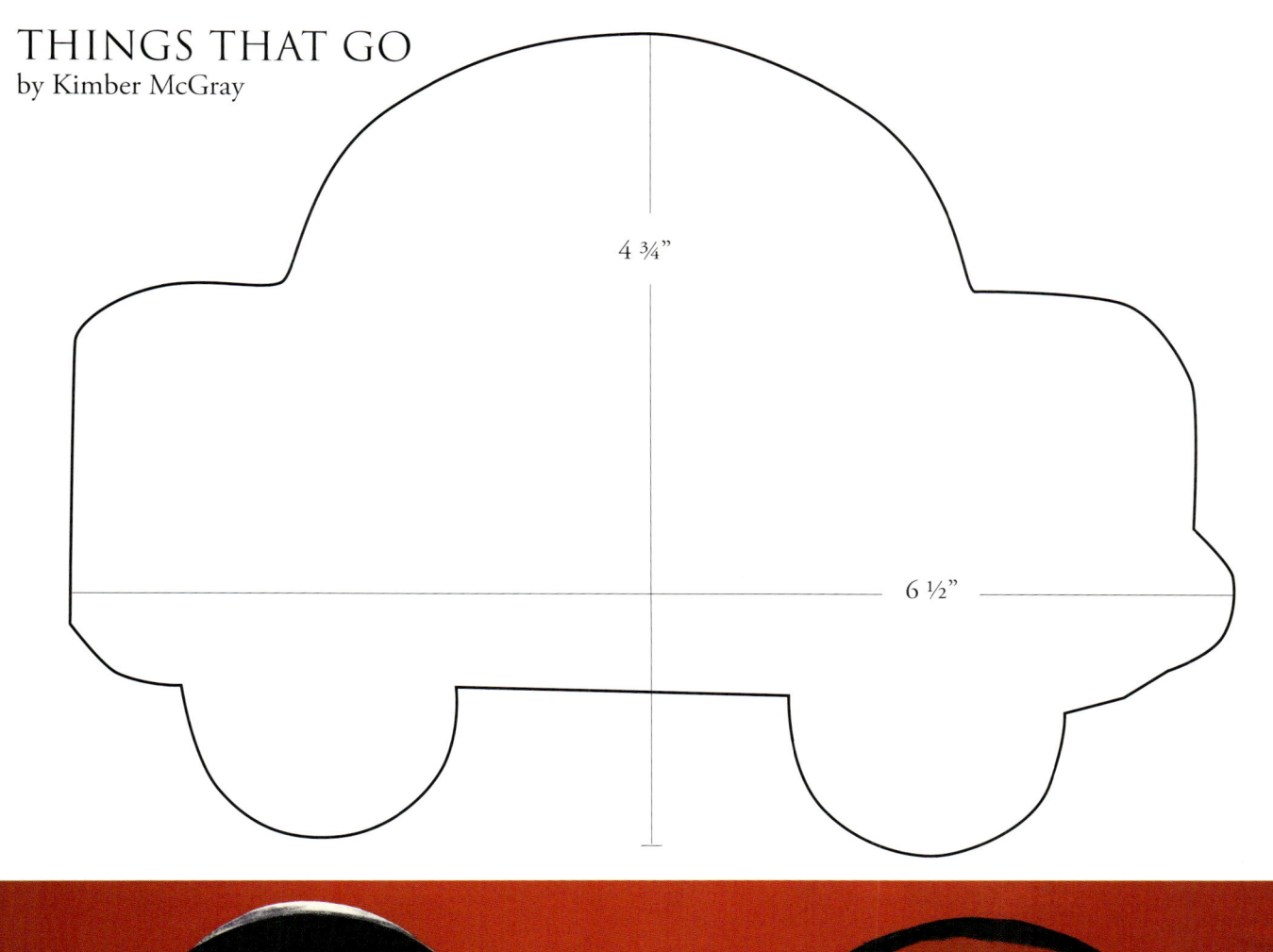

4 ¾"

6 ½"

Another year older and time to "move" up.
Come and see the next step in BIG kid wheels…

Peek under the hood of the car

Album is 6 ¾ x 4 ½"

Cardstock: Bazzill Basics; Patterned paper: Scenic Route Paper Co.; Brads: Making Memories; Metal embellishments: Basic Grey (bookplate), Maya Road (bottlecaps); Chipboard book, templates: Maya Road; Gems: EK Success; Tags: Autumn Leaves; Stickers: Making Memories; Ink: Ranger; Pens: Uni-Ball Signo, Zig; Marker: Stampin' Up!

To create the peek-a-boo flaps, Kimber cut flaps in certain parts of the car (door, hood, window, etc.) with an x-acto knife, scoring one of the four sides so it would open neatly. She adhered a photograph on the next page and then adhered the two pages together. Voila—when you open the flap, you see the picture! After the pages were done, she used the Crop-a-Dile by We R Memory Keepers to punch holes in the chipboard so it could be held together with binder rings. She also punched holes for the wheels, drilled through bottle caps with a ¼" drill bit and fastened the bottle cap wheels with brads.

 What do pastels, practical jokes and basketball have in common? They are my 13-year-old daughter's passions. I love looking at this little book because the photos celebrate Isabel's essence at this stage in her life. Mini books are a great way to unify photos taken at different events—in this case I have collected pictures of her coming home from basketball camp as an 'All-Star,' volunteering to be the 'Cheetoh-head' at a 4th of July picnic, and of her art work created with pastels. The heart shaped cover and pages match the 'Do What You Love' theme."

DO WHAT YOU LOVE
by Miriam Campbell

Album is 3 ¼ x 4"
Ribbon: Heidi Grace Designs, Offray; Chipboard, die cuts, rub ons, stickers: Heidi Grace Designs; Pen: Sharpie; Craft drill: Fiskars

Miram wanted to create an album about her 13-year old daughter's passions: pastels, basketball, and practical jokes. She used a large chipboard heart by Heidi Grace as a cover and as a template for the pages. Punch holes in the corner (or use a drill as Miriam did) and bind the pages together with a ring.

"I wanted to capture my son's first year of preschool. I didn't have a lot of photos, but the ones I had were great, so a mini album was the perfect way to go. I love having all the stories and memories from that year all together to look back on."

MY SCHOOL YEAR by Greta Hammond

Album is 6 ½" square
Cardstock: Bazzill Basics; Patterned paper, twill, die cuts: Autumn Leaves, Foof-a-La; Brads: Making Memories; Photo turns, gaffer tape: 7 Gypsies; Felt: Memories Complete; Chipboard: Heidi Swapp; Rub ons: Autumn Leaves, Making Memories; Stickers: EK Success, Karen Foster Design; Binder rings: Office Max; Ink: Ranger; Paint: Delta; Font: Times New Roman; Envelope: Li'l Davis Designs

Greta used school-themed products throughout the album to give it a cohesive feel. She made the closure on the cover from twill and a buckle from a pair of overalls. The book is interactive, with pull-out journaling and a file folder which opens to reveal scanned progress reports. Very creative!

You probably made close to fifty different craft projects this year at preschool. Each one unique in their own way. Each one carefully displayed on the refrigerator. But I have to say, this was my favorite. When you walked out with it on, I was laughing so hard that I almost drove up on the curb. I just thought it was the funniest thing. You wore it proudly on Thanksgiving day.

TURKEY HAT

CRAFT
REPORT

LEARN

PROGRESS

67890

LAST DAY
REPORT

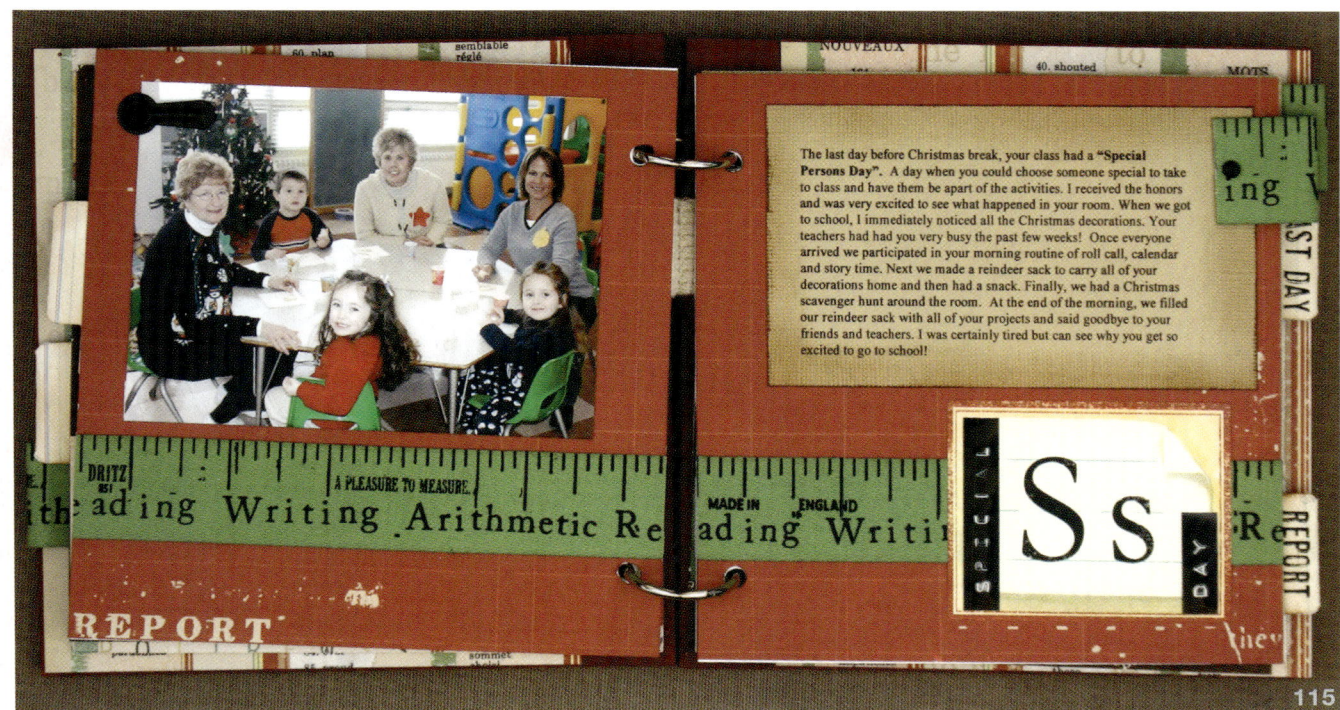

The last day before Christmas break, your class had a **"Special Persons Day"**. A day when you could choose someone special to take to class and have them be apart of the activities. I received the honors and was very excited to see what happened in your room. When we got to school, I immediately noticed all the Christmas decorations. Your teachers had had you very busy the past few weeks! Once everyone arrived we participated in your morning routine of roll call, calendar and story time. Next we made a reindeer sack to carry all of your decorations home and then had a snack. Finally, we had a Christmas scavenger hunt around the room. At the end of the morning, we filled our reindeer sack with all of your projects and said goodbye to your friends and teachers. I was certainly tired but can see why you get so excited to go to school!

 "I had no idea that cheerleading was so much work until my little sister, Amy, decided to give it a try. They practice most of the summer and cheer all through the year, with early morning practices every day before school. It was fun to create this quick & simple book to help her record some of her high school memories, and to let her know how proud I am of her and how much I love her."

AMY by Tammy Morrill

free spirits
PRECIOUS
UNFORGETTABLE
THRILLED
energy
pizzaz
groovy
TOGETHER

Michelle & Amy...
VARSITY CHEER
2006-2007

go

team!

WOW the CROWD!

CHEER Squad

HALF-TIME

mhs

Album is 10 ½" square
Album, flower: Making Memories; Cardstock: Bazzill Basics; Patterned paper, letter stickers, pen: American Crafts; Rhinestone brad: SEI; Ribbon: May Arts; Flower stamp: Cactus Pink; Letter stamps: Green Grass Stamps; Ink: Stampin' Up!

Tammy stamped her sister's name and a flower in red on a pink insert, then fastened the white blossom in place through both the plastic protector and the paper underneath with a rhinestone brad.

 Field Day is an annual function at my daughter's school. Family and friends are invited and the girls spend the school week prior preparing for the event and making t-shirts. The events of the day include a mass, parade, field events, and a picnic. I had a great time creating a mini album to document this fun tradition."

FIELD DAY by Laura O'Donnell

Album is 6 ¾ x 3 ¼"

Patterned paper, ribbon, chipboard, die cuts, stickers: SEI; Rub ons: Making Memories; Tag Album: 7 Gypsies; Pens: Zig

Laura converted all of her photos to black and white and added a splash of color with paper and embellishments from the SEI Penelope's Potpourri collection. She decoupaged paper to the inside and outside covers of the album, then used regular adhesive for the inside pages. Notice her simple formula of placing a photo every right side, and embellishments and journaling on the left.

This was a fun one—they ran to the circle, took off shoes, then ran back, found their shoes & put them back on again.

Our Principal, Sister Mary Ellen, and V.P. Sister Steven Ann

Second graders on parade! After the family Mass the girls paraded out and the games got started.

READY!

SET!

DONE!

1 HOUR ALBUM!

Find citrus kick 6 x 6 box kit at your local scrapbook or craft store.
One hour albums are avaliable in many other themes and sizes.

" I decided last year that creating mini books was the route I wanted to take when it came to my own personal journal. My children can look through them and see a glimpse of their mother, the relationship between their parents and my personal thoughts about them as my children. This album is for the special everyday moments of 2006."

"I love to use crystals on my layouts and albums, and now Swarvoski Crystals come with adhesive on the back (look for 'Crystal Fire' on the packaging). I also use the BeJeweler by Crystal Innovations to apply my crystals; both can be purchased at Michaels for a reasonable price. I've applied these crystals to transparencies, felt, chipboard, flowers… pretty much anything you can think of!"

2006 by Dedra Long

Album is 7 ½ x 7 ¼"

Album, decorative tape, twist tie: 7 Gypsies; Patterned paper: 7 Gypsies, Creative Imaginations, Foof-a-La, Making Memories, Melissa Frances; Mini file folder: Foof-a-La; Chipboard, colored pencils, ghost rectangle: Heidi Swapp; Metal embellishments: Nunn Designs; Flowers: 7 Gypsies, American Crafts, Heidi Swapp, Prima; Die cuts: Paper Source; Buttons: Foof-a-La, Swarovski; Crystals, jewels: Swarovski; Rub ons: 7 Gypsies, Autumn Leaves, Basic Grey; Stickers: 7 Gypsies, Making Memories; Ribbon: May Arts; Tags: Jenni Bowlin Studios; Napkin: Target; Gift card: Starbucks; Transparency frame: My Mind's Eye; Stamps: 7 Gypsies, Autumn Leaves, Fontwerks, Making Memories, Stampin' Up!, Technique Tuesday, Inkadinkado; Ink: ColorBox, StazOn, Tsukineko; Pens: Ranger, Zig; Marker: Sharpie; Other: Transparency, antique knob, paper doilies; Photography: Dedra Long, Heidi Swapp

The decorative swirls on Dedra's cover look like they were stamped directly onto the patterned paper, but they're actually stamped on a transparency, attached over the paper, then decorated with jewels. Look closely to notice how Dedra finds uses for a lot of household items to beautify her album, such as an antique drawer pull on the cover.

2005

you are one of my nicest thoughts · georgia o'keefe · i love you just the way you are · billy joel | beginnings

the last moments of 2005... one of the last pictures taken of you and me... we have grown so much this year... discovering ourselves and loving each other throughout our journey... some people believe or like to make resolutions for the new year... this year I wanted to take a moment & this picture to capture US... you & me...

i live for those who love me, for those who know me true. · george linnaeus banks | relationships · cre

2006

haven   but whatever road you choose, I'm right behind you, win or lose · bob dylan | laughter   fun

this was one of the first pictures of 2006... you being funny... "come on honey, lets take a picture"... secretly I think you likes capturing moments just as much as I do... Welcome to 2006... a new year of hope, struggle, finding our way together... you, us and our two girls... I will always be by your side... the two of us together...   love U..!

our tribe   lean upon me, i'll lean upon you, we'll be ok · dave matthews   kinship   fabric of our lives

i remember...

I remember the first time I saw you.... at that time we were both working in the corporate world.... I saw you across the room as you were shutting the blinds that were by your desk.... It was like yesterday that I noticed you and felt that warm, fuzzy feeling....At that exact moment I knew that you would become my husband one day...And here we are 7 years later together husband & wife... I ♥ U.... me....

4.06

everyday you are pulled a million different directions... I tell you all the time how much you inspire me & how awesome you

u

J

...you pick up the phone all day...

...are with people...

this ✿ door

This way

this door represents ..... your *Passion*, your dream ... a partnership and trust with your dad ... a family business ... you walk through this door everyday with new possibilities and immense opportunity ... this door would not exist without you behind it ... this door has the love & joy life inside it everyday ...

2006
JAN JUL
FEB AUG
MAR SEPT
APR OCT
MAY NOV
JUN DEC

upgrade
DESIGN. LLC

dream
inspire
believe

she said

12.31.06

you both inspire and influence my life everyday I love u both ...

LOOKING WITH MY HEART

COPYRIGHT© 6.04

COPYRIGHT© 12.06

Every time I look at this picture it brings so many emotions up inside me ... When I took this picture I remember being so proud of my two beautiful daughters ... Vai was eight years old and Ellie was 18 months! ... Shelby took Ellie's hand and guided her down the path ... Shelby was talking and showing things to Ellie as they were walking ... my girls, discovering the world around them together ... I did not have a sister but this picture tells my heart that my girls love each other and will always be there for one another ... Ellie took Shelby's hand with no hesitation ... they trust each other with no question ... Shelby has always protected Ellie since the day she was born ... I'm a proud mama knowing they have each other!

"I am always looking for ways to stay organized, so I designed this 'balance book' as a way to keep track of my spending. I created the balance sheets in Microsoft Word, so I can print refill pages as needed. I also included a vellum pocket to store receipts that are waiting to be filed. Now I have a simple and fun way to stay on top of my finances. So you might ask: where *does* it all go? I think we all know the answer: scrapbooking supplies!"

WHERE DOES IT ALL GO?

by Andrea Beaumont

Album is 6 x 4 ¾"
Patterned paper: KI Memories; Vellum envelope: Unknown; Ribbon: Michaels; Chipboard: KI Memories (arrow), Maya Road ("$"); Stickers: EK Success; Embossing enamel: Ranger; Paint: Plaid; Font: CK Road Trip; Other: Binding coil

Andrea painted the chipboard dollar sign with white pearl paint to match the frosted finish of the paper, then heat embossed it with Ultra Thick Embossing Enamel for added dimension. Instead of discarding a leftover strip from the bottom of her patterned paper, Andrea used it as an accent on the cover. Notice how the colorful little circles and the barcode really tie the finance theme together.

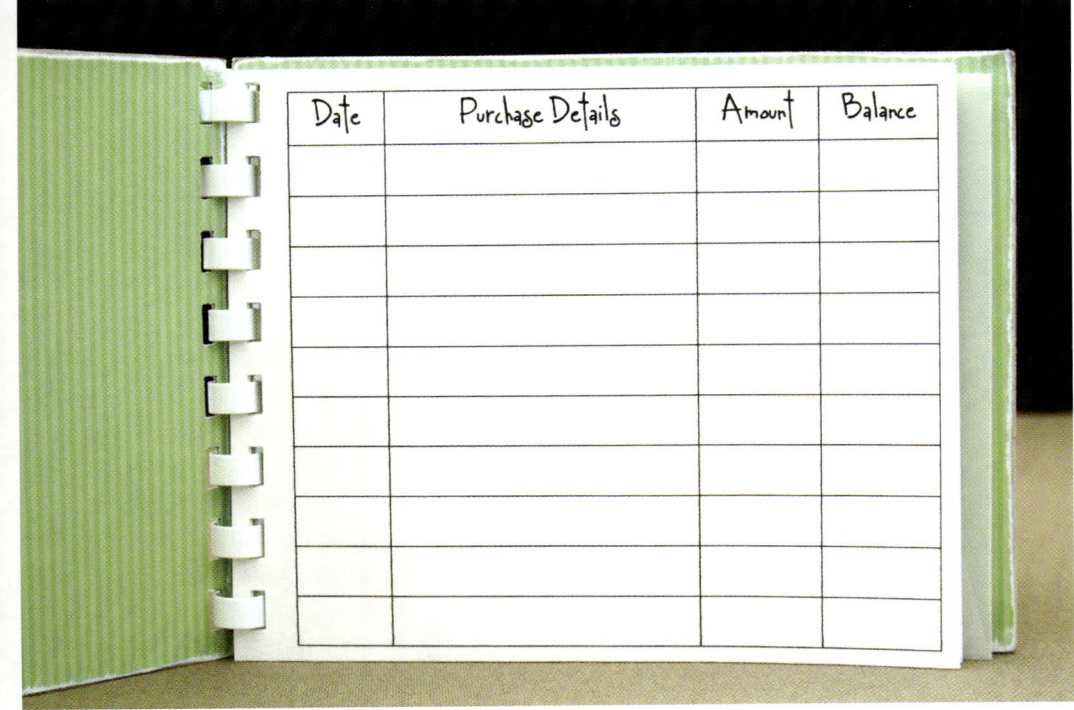

Date	Purchase Details	Amount	Balance

"As I entered this new year, I wanted to really focus on getting healthy. I have been trying to lose weight for years with little to no success. But as I am getting older and my boys are growing up, I want to be able to do this—not just for myself, but for my husband and my boys. To help make my weight loss goals a reality, I decided to create a journal to document my thoughts and feelings throughout this journey. I also created a rewards book to track my progress and give myself encouragement. I set rewards in five pound increments, and that has worked really well for me."

WEIGHT LOSS NOTEBOOKS by Chrys Queen Rose

Weight Album is 7 ½ x 9 ¾", Weight Loss Rewards Album is 6 ¼ x 3"
Cardstock: Bazzill Basics; Patterned paper, epoxy flower: Autumn Leaves; Ribbon: Unknown; Chipboard: Heidi Swapp; Buttons: Foof-a-La; Rub ons: American Crafts; Stickers: American Crafts (foam), Boxer Scrapbook Productions; Rubber band book: 7 Gypsies; Composition book: Office supply

Chrys decorated a composition book for her journaling and a rubber band album from 7 Gypsies to list her rewards based on amount of weight lost. She makes it very appealing to look through by using fun and vibrant patterned papers and embellishments. Other rewards include: 10 pounds - Day at the Spa, 20 pounds - New hair cut and color, 30 pounds - New pair of Designer Jeans!

i'M expecting!

I'm Feeling

The Big News

Pregnancy

Journal

" The inspiration for this journal was to share and preserve the exciting memories and emotions that come with bringing a new baby into the world. From hearing the big news to going through the various stages of pregnancy, moms-to-be will be glad they started this tradition—it will be a lot of fun to share with your child when he or she is older. Consider adding more pages and topics that will make the album unique to you: a list of baby names you are considering, a letter to baby about your hopes and dreams for them, etc."

I'M EXPECTING
by Close To My Heart

Album is 5 x 7"
All products by Close To My Heart except Coluzzle File Folder template
Cardstock: Breeze; Patterned paper: Groovy Blossoms; Brads: White Daisy
My Accents; Ribbon: White Daisy Ribbon Rounds; Chipboard: Dimensional
Elements Bookplates; Stamps: My Acrylix Stamp Set: Expecting; Ink: Cocoa

Kellie created this compact album using three small colorful file folders
decorated with patterned paper and bound together with brown cardstock.
Each folder has label prompts on the tabs to get your writing flowing,
including "The Big News," "I'm Feeling..." and "Getting Ready."

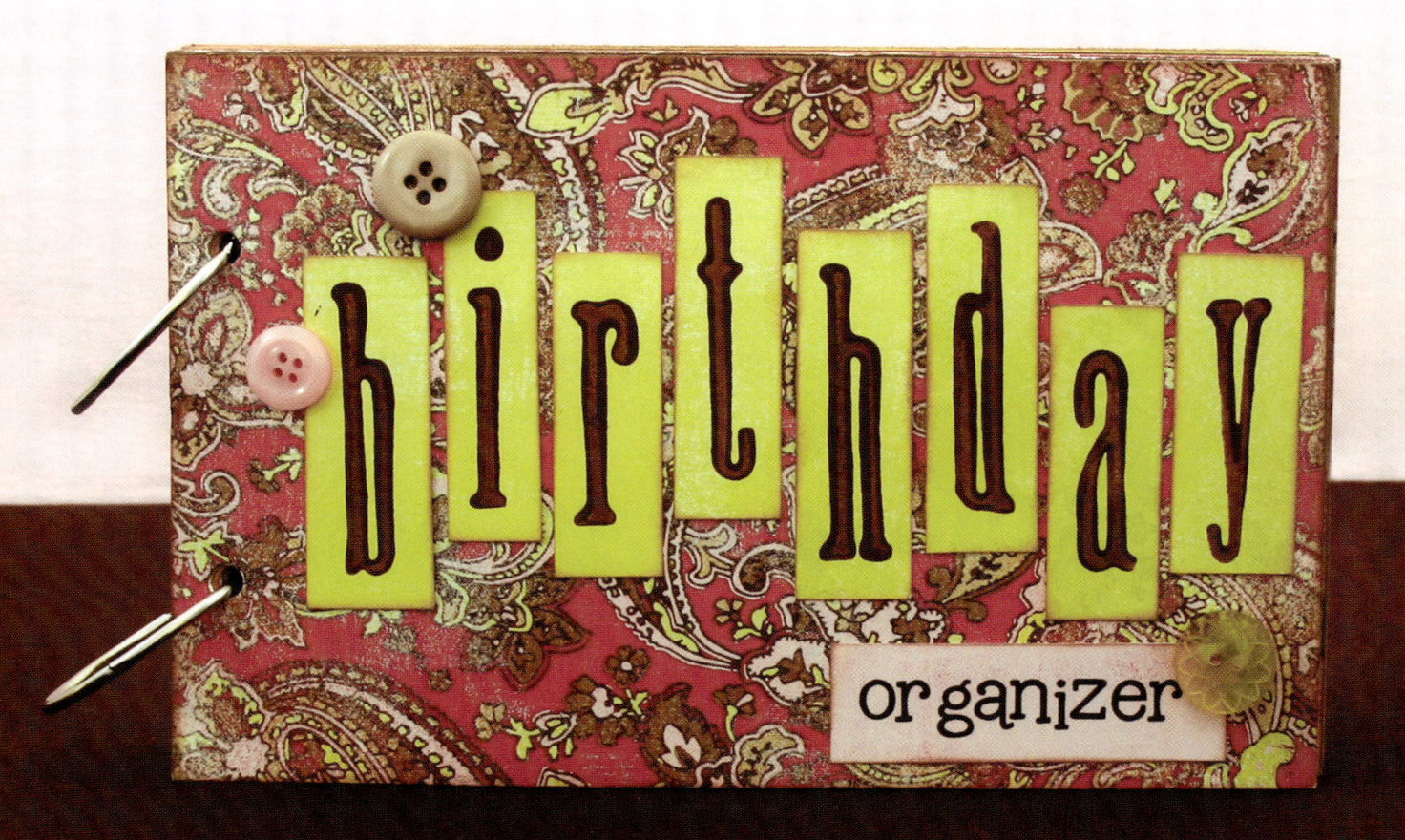

 I wanted to have a central location to keep track of birthdays and anniversaries—one book where all the dates were located, so I wouldn't have to transfer them to a new planner each year. This organizer has a section for each month where I write down the important names/dates on little strips of paper (so it's easy to add more names as needed). I also included a manila envelope for each month to store blank birthday/anniversary cards, which makes sending off a card on time really simple!"

BIRTHDAY ORGANIZER by Laura Vegas

Album is 9 ½ x 6"
Patterned paper: My Mind's Eye; Brads, stamps: Making Memories; Ribbon: Offray; Chipboard: Craft supply; Buttons: Buttons Galore and More; Calendar template: Microsoft Works; Ink: Rubber Stampede; Paint: Delta; Pens: American Crafts; Font: 2Peas High Tide, from Autumn Leaves 15 Font CD; Other: Manila envelopes, metal rings

This chipboard album is the ultimate birthday planner—it lasts from year to year and has a folder to keep cards handy! For each month Laura has included a calendar on the left, a "tag page" with people's names on the right, and a manila envelope sandwiched in between. She used coordinating patterned paper from My Mind's Eye throughout to give the book a consistent feel.

 I often come across a great quote or idea that I want to use in my projects and I needed a book where I could gather all those random thoughts, as well as sketches I make for future layouts and the cute things my daughter says that I don't want to forget. I am an organizer, so this book is a way to help me stay organized when it comes to my scrapbooking."

IDEAS, THOUGHTS, SKETCHES AND QUOTES by Maadhavi Reddi

Album is 4 x 5 ½"
Patterned paper: Scenic Route Paper Co.; Chipboard: Li'l Davis Designs; Stickers: Heidi Swapp; Font: Lisa Bearnson's Font CD;
Notebook: Unknown

Maadhavi created this book as part of a Design Team assignment for Scrapbook Sussies. Notice how she layered two flowers cut from patterned paper on the cover, raising one with a foam dot to create even more dimension and depth.

 I made this album because I wanted something simple, elegant and beautiful to have out for visitors to enjoy. I didn't want it to be complicated, just a very sweet album about my youngest daughter."

MAC BOXED ALBUM by Keisha Campbell

Album is 7 x 4"
Patterned paper: Autumn Leaves; Ribbon: Unknown; Chipboard: Heidi Swapp, Melissa Frances; Flowers: Doodlebug Design, Prima; Buttons: Craft supply; Rub ons: Art Warehouse; Stamps: Stampin' Up!; Ink: StazOn; Scalloped scissors: Fiskars; Fonts: Times New Roman, unknown; Other: Rhinestones

Keisha wanted this album to capture a moment in time, because tomorrow those moments will be "bits & pieces of yesterday." She used rub on phrases over her photographs and stitched simple captions opposite the photos.

 I created this mini album to help me remember the crazy, everyday things my son does that make me smile. The pictures were taken throughout the year with no theme other than the fun things my little guy does. I love the pictures of him just being himself: silly, goofy, sometimes even sweet. It was a great way to showcase the different sides of my son's personality. This pocket sized mini album fits perfectly inside the tin, is great to toss into my purse or bag, and easy enough to make another copy for the grandparents."

A BOY'S POINT OF VIEW
by Kimber McGray

Album is 2 ¾ x 4"
Cardstock: Bazzill Basics; Patterned paper, decorative tape, coaster rings: Gin-X; Eyelets: We R Memory Keepers; Pen: Zig; Metal ring: Office Max; Tin: Provo Craft

Kimber set up her mini album so that each photograph has an introduction on the previous page, making it flow like a story. She used eyelets as hole reinforcers for color and stability.

 My inspiration for this brag book came from two needs: A calendar for my purse and a better way to carry around pictures of my girls. I love the idea of seeing their sweet faces every time I check a date! This blue and brown paper from Paper Salon was perfect for my project, but I wanted to add a little more color to make it pop. Matting the photos and calendars in red helped them stand out better on the pages. The extra red embellishments, like the button and heart, helped tie it all together. To help the silver snowflake charm on the first page stand out, I heat embossed it red. I printed 'smile' on a scratch piece of paper, then used temporary adhesive to hold the tag in place over it while I ran it through the printer again."

BRAG BOOK by Lisa Dorshey

Album is 2 ¾ x 4"

Cardstock: Worldwin; Patterned paper, tags: Paper Salon; Charms: Making Memories; Metal embellishments: Li'l Davis Designs (binder clip), Scrapworks (circle clip); Ribbon: American Crafts, Li'l Davis Designs, unknown; Magnets: Basic Grey; Chipboard: Heidi Swapp; Flowers: American Crafts, Prism; Buttons: Unknown; Stickers: American Stickers, Paper Salon; Embossing powder: Stampendous; Diary cover: Self-Addressed; Ink: ColorBox; Paint: Plaid; Pen: Zig; Font: Adorable, from dafont.com; Calendars: Calendarsthatwork.com

Lisa keeps the cover securely closed with a magnet under the top flap. She accents her pages with adorable embellishments, like the snowflake charm that she heat embossed in sparkling red peeking out from behind the January calendar.

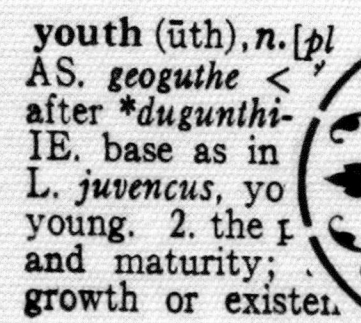

youth (ūth), *n*. [*pl* ūthz)], [ME. *youthe*; AS. *geoguthe* < *nthi* with *g* for *w* after *dugunthi- ones, veterans)]; IE. base as in actly parallel to L. *juvencus*, yo quality of being young. 2. the p etween childhood and maturity; n early stage of growth or existen people collectively.

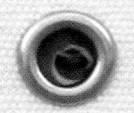

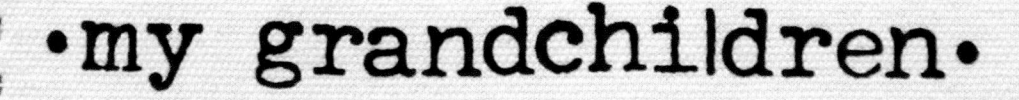 •my grandchildren•

 I love dictionaries, encyclopedias, and text books, and often try to include pages from these books in my layouts. If you aren't worried about reading the book later, you can include the actual page, or you can simply scan the page and print it on cardstock. Dictionaries are particularly fun, because you can include the portion that describes your subject. For example, I used part of an 'M' page with the word 'magic' to describe my niece, Mia."

MY GRANDCHILDREN by Betsy Sammarco

Album is 7 x 4"
Patterned paper: My Mind's Eye; Chipboard: Bazzill Basics, Making Memories; Circle punch: Marvy Uchida; Rub ons: Creative Imaginations, Making Memories; Font: Times New Roman; Dictionary: Random House; Tag book: Creative Imaginations

To create the custom rub on embellishment on her cover, Betsy first applied the circle rub on, then cut a slightly larger circle from the definition rub on with an x-acto knife, then applied the definition rub on around the circle.

 I don't seem to get around to handing out pictures of my girls to their grandparents during the year, so each Christmas I make them mini albums containing some of my favorite pictures from the past year. Last year I enjoyed learning more about photography and felt the pictures could stand on their own, so I kept the album simple with the focus on the photos. I was able to make four of these albums with one pack of patterned paper and one pack of cardstock."

ALYSSA & SARAH by Laura Vegas

Album is 8 x 7"
Cardstock: Bazzill Basics; Patterned paper: Basic Grey; Brads, metal embellishments, flowers, page pebbles: Making Memories; Ribbon: Making Memories, Offray; Circle cutter: Creative Memories; Die cuts: Doodlebug Design, QuicKutz; Font: Elise, from momscorner4kids.com

For a soft touch, Laura used a leather flower on the cover of her album. Clear page pebbles from Making Memories are a great way to embellish flower centers.

 This little book about our cat is very special to me. We got her when our 19-year-old cat passed away; she is a hurricane Katrina survivor that was rescued from New Orleans and brought to Washington State with several other animals. I always want to remember these fun things about her personality."

OUR NEW LITTLE CAT

by Alissa Fast

Album is 7 x 6"
Patterned paper, metal embellishments, rub ons: Karen Foster Design; Chipboard: Craft supply, Heidi Swapp; Die cuts: AccuCut; Stickers: Karen Foster Design, Making Memories; Ink: Ranger; Paint: Making Memories; Pen: Zig; Binder rings: Office supply

Alissa's album pages are AccuCut die cuts, which she hole punched and bound with binder rings. Each page was painted around the edges and then embellished. She used Heidi Swapp ghost letters as templates for the patterned paper "our cat" letters on the cover.

aka: batman & patch

max & duke

After these two precocious puppies entered our lives, they kept my husband and I awake at night for about 8 weeks. First, it was whining, then it was scratching at their box and finally, it was the ability to climb out of the box. We gave them temporary names so we could differentiate them in our conversation. Patch was the mild mannered one and Batman was the ferocious, playful one. When we gave them away in December, it was a sad day, but definitely a relief! They went to two families who love them so much and who also gave them respectable names: Max and Duke."

MAX & DUKE by April Foster

Album is 6 x 2"
Cardstock: Bazzill Basics; Stickers: 7 Gypsies, American Crafts, Scrapworks; Stamps, pen: Stampin' Up!; Ink: Tsukineko

April created this skinny flipbook out of five 6 x 2" strips of white Bazzill Basics cardstock. She bound the pages together with strips of masking tape, and covered the left pages with 4 x 6" photos cut in half horizontally.

life is about loving...

Unconditional

friendship

life

"I've been involved with dog rescue for the past 12 years and was inspired to do this little album as a way to remember all the things my foster dogs have taught me. I copied all of my pictures in Microsoft Word and used text boxes to create the journaling right on the pictures. I wanted to use bright and colorful embellishments, so I kept my pictures black and white. The base of this book is a children's board book."

UNCONDITIONAL FRIENDSHIP by Cheryl Baase

Album is 7 x 7 ½"
Cardstock: Bazzill Basics; Patterned paper, ribbon: KI Memories; Chipboard: Maya Road; Rub ons: Basic Grey; Stickers: KI Memories, unknown; Overlays: My Mind's Eye; Pen: Zig; Markers: Sharpie; Font: Unknown

Cheryl adds a personal and unique touch to her album with doodling. Notice all the intricate doodles throughout the pages including on the pictures, flowers, and as their own accents.

 Mary Rose (my 7-year old daughter) and I made this book together. I had just come home from shopping and showed her these great cat-themed papers and stickers I'd bought. When she saw them, she wanted to make something with them immediately! We gathered all of the pictures of our cat, Koba, that we could find and we used them as they were—a mix of color and black and white. We had photos from when he was a kitten and pictures of him now and allowed the papers and phrases on the stickers guide how we put the book together. I stamped the journaling spots and let my daughter write the journaling because I love getting her handwriting at different ages in our scrapbooks. It was a quick, fun project that came together in just a couple hours."

PURRFECT PALS by Laura O'Donnell

Album is 4 ¼ x 6"
Cardstock, ink: Stampin' Up!; Patterned paper, stickers, mini album: Rusty Pickle; Fish clip, fibers: Unknown; Stamps: Fontwerks, Technique Tuesday (cat words); Pen: Zig; Other: Mod Podge

Get your kids involved in making mini albums with you! When you're done, you'll have a great finished product and a fun memory to boot.

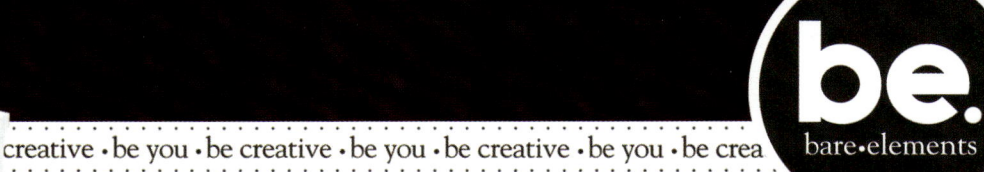

Metropolis

Lively geometrics and a clean, crisp color palette make **Metropolis** 'out of this world'! The retro, funky designs paired with cool blues, greens and oranges are the perfect combination for your next summertime project.

Come check out our **brand new website**! Visit the layout gallery, enter to win Scenic Route product and sign up for the Scenic Route Newsletter!

www.scenicroutepaper.com

Scenic Route

INDEX OF DESIGNERS

RETAIL STORE DIRECTORY

ONLINE STORE DIRECTORY

ALLY SCRAPS
www.allyscraps.com

BLESSINGS RECEIVED
www.stores.ebay.com/blessings-received

EXPRESSIVE SCRAPBOOKS
www.expressivescrapbooks.com

UNDERGROUND SCRAPBOOKING SUPPLY CO.
COEURD' ALENE, ID
208-664-6010
originalsbygina@hotmail.com
www.OBGunderground.com

SCRAP HAPPY KT
PO BOX 436
ELDERSBURG, MA 21784
410-549-3222

THE SCRAP STOP
www.thescrapstop.com

URBAN SCRAPPER
www.urbanscrapperonline.com

WE STASH IT, SO YOU DON'T HAVE TO!
951-245-7187
www.yourscrapbookstash.com

ARIZONA

BINDING MEMORIES BY IDA
1150 DUCE OF CLUBS STE C
SHOWLOW, AZ 85901
(928) 537-8116

PAPER & METAL SCRAPPERS
804 B. NORTH BEELINE HWY
SWISS VILLAGE SHOPS
PAYSON, AZ 85541
928-468-1188
paperandmetal@earthlink.net

CALIFORNIA

PAGES IN TYME
560 PINE KNOTT BLVD STE B
BIG BEAR LAKE, CA 92315
909-866-3661
M-S 10-6 SUN 10-5

SCRAPBOOK BLESSINGS
1560 NEWBURY ROAD STE 5
NEWBURY PARK, CA 91320
805-375-1568
M-Sat 9-6
service@scrapbookblessings.com
www.scrapbookblessings.com

SCRAPBOOK NOOK
444 SAN MATEO AVE.
SANBRUNO, CA 94066
650-588-3112

STAMPERS WAREHOUSE
101-G TOWN & COUNTRY DR
DANVILLE, CA 94526
(925) 362-9595

TABLE SCRAPZ
2500 E. IMPERIAL HWY SUITE 136
BREA, CA 92821
(714) 529-6887
M-F 11-7, SAT 10-6 SUN 11-5
customerservice@tablescrapz.com

COLORADO

STAMPING TO SEE YOU
8019 S JOHNSON CT
LITTLETON, CO 80128
303-932-6795
www.stampingtoseeyou.com

THE TREASURE BOX
1833 E. HARMONY RD #1
FORT COLLINS, CO 80528
970-207-9939
M-F 9:30-6 TH 9:30-9
SAT 10-5

CONNECTICUT

NEW ENGLAND SCRAPBOOK CO
200 ALBANY TURNPIKE-RTE 44
CANTON, CT 06019
860-693-9197
M-tu 10-6 W-th 10-9 F-sat 10-10 Sun 12-6
www.newenglandscrapbook.com

FLORIDA

CROPPIN' CORNER
175-C NE EGLIN PKWY
FT.WALTON BEACH, FL 32548
850-581-2767
M ,W-F 9-6 TUE 9-8 SAT 9-5
www.croppincornerfl.com

MY PRECIOUS MEMORIES
5566 S. FLAMINGO RD.
COOPER CITY, FL 33330

RUBAN ROUGE
3454 TAMPA ROAD
PALM HARBOR, FL 34684
727-784-8600
info@rubanrougepaperarts.com
rubanrougepaperarts.com

GEORGIA

SCRAPBOOK OUTLET
PRIME OUTLET S-CALHOUN #90
CALHOUN, GA 30701
706-602-3555
I-75, EXIT 312, 40 ML N OF ATLANTA
Scrapbookoutlet.com

HAWAII

SCRAPBOOK CLUBHOUSE HAWAII
98-302 KAMEHAMEHA HWY
AIEA, HI 96701
808-486-0333
JUST 5 MINS FROM PEARL HARBOR
M 10-3, T-SAT 10-7 SUN 11-3
www.scrapbookclubhousehawaii.com

THE SCRAPPERS' DEN
719 KAMEHAMEHA HWY SUITE C201
PEARL CITY, HI 96782
808-455-4100
T-FR 10-6, SAT 10-4 SUN 11-3
www.scrappersden.com

IDAHO

CINDY'S
34 NORTH MAIN STREET
MALAD, ID 83252
208-766-2666
www.cindysscrapbooking.com

**A SCRAPPERS
& STAMPERS DELIGHT**
TIFFANY SQUARE
156 MAIN AVE N.
TWIN FALLS, ID 83301
208-736-7286
mary@scrapthatsmile.com
www.scrapthatsmile.com

CINDY'S
34 NORTH MAIN ST
MALAD, ID 83252
208-766-2666
www.cindysscrapbooking.com

ILLINOIS

MEMORIES & BEYOND
1400 C 75TH STREET
DOWNERS GROVE, IL 60516
630-271-0610
M-F 10-9, SAT 10-6, SUN 12-5
CROP NIGHT, FRI & SAT
info@memoriesbeyond.com
www.memoriesbeyond.com
www.yourscrapbookcorner.com

SCRAP N STAMP ART
901 SOUTH NEIL ST, STE B
CHAMPAIGN, IL 61820
217-352-0532
M-F 10-6, SAT 10-5, SUN 11-5
www.scrapnstampart.com

SCRAPBOOK SOURCE
557 W. NORTH AVE.
CHICAGO, IL 60610
312-440-9720
M-F 10-8, SAT 10-6, SUN 12-5
CROP NIGHT, FRIDAY
info@scrapbooksourceinc.com
www.scrapbooksourceinc.com
www.yourscrapbookcorner.com

INDIANA

SCHMITT PHOTO
4847 PLAZA EAST BLVD
EVANSVILLE, IN 47715
812-473-0245
M-F 8:30-8 SAT 9-6 SUN 1-5
www.schmittphoto.com

SCRAPAHOLICS
811 W. McGALLIARD RD.
MUNCIE, IN 47303
765-213-9900
M-F 10-6, SAT 9-4
www.scrapaholics1.com

SCRAPBOOK OUTLET
PRIME OUTLET- FREMONT #10
FREMONT, IN 46737
260-833-2767
I-69 AND 80/90 TOLL ROAD
Luv2scrapbook.com

SCRAPBOOK XANADU
520 N. STATE RD #135
GREENWOOD, IN 46142
317-885-7200
M-F 10-9 SAT 10-7 SUN 12-5
www.scrapbookxanadu.com

KENTUCKY

SCRAPBOOK OUTLET
DRY RIDGE OUTLET CENTER #1106
DY RIDGE, KY 41035
859-823-2767
I-75 25 ML S. OF CINCINNATI
Scrapbookoutlet.com

MAINE

MEMORY LANE
20 COBURN ST
AUBURN, ME 04210
207-782-1600
memorylanepages@aol.com
www.memorylanepages.com

MY CROP PAPER SCISSOR STORE
168 FRONT STREET
FARMINGTON, ME 04938
207-778-6660
TUE- FR 9-5:30, SAT & SUN 10-4
www.mycpsstore.com

MARYLAND

SCRAP HAPPY KT
PO BOX 436
ELDERSBURG, MD 21784
410-549-3222
www.scraphappykt.com

MASSACHUSETTS

LEAVE A LEGACY SCRAPBOOKING
1510 NEW STATE HWY RT 44 UNIT 18
RAYNHAM, MA 02767
508-880-6900
M-CLOSED, T-TH 10-8,
W,F,SAT 10-6 SUN 12-4
www.leavealegacyscrapbooking .com

MICHIGAN

PAGES IN TIME
6323 C WEST SAGINAW HWY
LANSING, MI 48917
517-327-5526

MINNESOTA

MEMORY BOX
38 N. UNION ST.
MORA, MN 55051
320-679-3439
www.memorybox.biz

MISSOURI

THE SCRAP OUTLET.COM
1320 W 40 HWY
ODESSA, MO 64076
816-230-5579
LOCATED AT THE ODESSA OUTLET MALL
www.thescrapoutlet.com
COME VISIT OUR WEB SITE FOR FREE OFFERS

NEVADA

PEBBLES IN MY POCKET
7650 W. SAHARA
LAS VEGAS, NV. 89117
702-438-9080
OPEN SEVEN DAYS A WEEK
www.pebbleslasvegas.com

NEW YORK

YOUR HAPPY PLACE
272 LARKFIELD RD
E. NORTHPORT, NY 11731
www.yourhappyplaceonline.com

NORTH CAROLINA

A PAGE IN TIME
1216-A PARKWAY DR.
GOLDSBORO, NC 27534
919-344-7884
Arlene@apgntime.com
www.apgntime.com

**ENCHANTED COTTAGE
RUBBER STAMP & SCRAPBOOKS**
JUST WEST OF WINSTON-SALEM
6275 SHALLOWFORD RD
LEWISVILLE, NC 27023
336-945-5889
M 10-3 T, W, F 10-5:30 TH 10-8 SAT 10-4
www.enchantedcottagenc.com

OHIO

**COUNTRY CROSSING
& CROPPERS CORNER**
IN FRONT OF WALMART
CORNER OF STATE RT 250
&WESTWIND DR
NORWALK,OH 44857
419-663-0496
postmaster@cropperscorner.net
www.cropperscorner.net

SCRAPBOOK OUTLET
PRIME OUTLETS- LODI #175
BURBANK, OHIO 44214
330-948-8080
I-71, EXIT 204, 20 ML S OF CLEVELAND
Scrapbookoutlet.com

OKLAHOMA

A SCRPABOOK GALLERY
12091 PERRY HWY STE 1
WEXFORD, PA 15090
724-933-9310
m-w 10-8, th 10-10, f-s 10-midnight sun 12-4
www.ascrapbookgallery.com

SCRAPBOOKS FROM THE HEART
11649 S. WESTERN AVE.
OKLAHOMA CITY, OK 73170
405-692-6491
M-S 10-6, SUN 1-5
www.scrapbooksfromtheheartokc.com

SCRAP HAPPYS
7142 S. MEMORIAL DR.
TULSA, OK 74133
918-250-0472
M-W, S 10-6 TH-F 10-8 SUN 1-5
www.scraphappys.com

OREGON

SCATTERED PICTURES
13852 NE SANDY BLVD
PORTLAND, OR 97230
503-252-1888
TU, TH,F- 10-5 W 10-8 SAT 10-4
CLOSED MON & SUN

SCRAP-A-DOODLE
354 NE NORTON SUITE 101
BEND, OR 97701
541-388-0311
scrap@scrap-a-doodle.com
www.scrap-a-doodle.com

PENNSYLVANIA

SCRAPBOOK SUPER STATION
A CRAFTERS HOME STORE
168 POINT PLAZA
BUTLER, PA 16001
724-287-4311
SUN 12-5 MON-SAT 10-9
www.scrapbookstation.com

TENNESSEE

THE CROP SHOP
7616 LEE HWY BLDG B
CHATTANOOGA, TN 37421
423-899-3515
store@cropshoponline.com
www.cropshoponline.com

TEXAS

**LONE STAR
SCRAPBOOK COMPANY**
27842 1-45 N.
THE WOOD LANDS, TX 77385
281-296-2296
www.lonestarscrapbook.com

NOVEL APPROACH
607 S FRIENDSWOOD DR.#15
FRIENDSWOOD, TX 77546
281-992-3137
www.novelapproachonline.com
info@novelapproachonline.com

SCRAPBOOK VILLAGE
3424 FM 1092 STE 270
MISSOURI CITY, TX 77459
281-208-5251
www.thescrapbookvillage.com

VERMONT

CREATIONS ABOUND
50 N. MAIN ST SUITE 101
ST ALBANS, VT 05478
TOLL FREE 877-517-3521
info@creationsabound.com
www.creationsabound.com

VIRGINIA

ALL ABOUT SCRAPBOOK
2137 UPTON DRIVE,STE 328
VIRGINIA BEACH, VA 23454
(RED MILLS COMMONS)
757-563-9009
www.allaboutscrapbooksonline.com

ADVERTISING DIRECTORY